# Oracle Certification Prep

Study Guide for

1Z0-071: Oracle Database 12c SQL

Matthew Morris

**Study Guide for Oracle Database 12c SQL (Exam 1Z0-071) Rev 1.0**

ODB PRESS
www.odbpress.com



ISBN-13: 978-1-941404-09-6
ISBN-10: 1-941404-09-X

# Table of Contents

## What to expect from the test

The test consists of 73 multiple choice or multiple answer questions and a duration of 100 minutes. With only 82 seconds per question you will need to be very careful of your time when taking this exam. The passing score listed on Oracle Education at this time is 63%, but as with all Oracle certification tests, they note it is subject to change.

To do well on the test you have to have a good grasp of SQL syntax rules. You'll also need to be able to utilize some common SQL functions, recognize the result of basic DDL operations, and know some of the facts regarding how SQL statements and functions are executed. Not all of the exhibits in the test are really crucial to answering the question being asked. You should read the question being asked before viewing the exhibit. If nothing else, reading the question first will provide you with information on what to look for in the exhibit, and it may allow you to skip viewing it entirely, giving you more time for other questions. Be sure to look at all of the answers before selecting what you think is the correct one. In some cases, more than one answer could be considered 'correct', but one of the two is a better answer. Also, it's valuable to look through the questions that contain SQL statements to find those with errors. Once you have eliminated those with obvious errors, you can concentrate on the remaining options to find the best solution.

Database administrators and developers tend to use SQL on a daily basis. If you do not currently know SQL well, this is not an area to skimp on. An Oracle professional with poor SQL skills will have serious and continuing problems fulfilling the job requirements of a DBA or developer. While you are preparing for this exam, take the time to really read up on the subject and practice writing SQL. This is knowledge that you will use. It is worth spending the time to learn as much as possible.

# What to Expect from this Study Guide

This document is built around the subject matter topics that Oracle Education has indicated will be tested. This book contains material from several Oracle documentation sources along with results from numerous SQL queries similar to what you'll see on the test. The guide covers a significant percentage of the information and operations that you must be familiar with in order to pass the exam.

What this guide is intended to do is to present the information that will be covered on the exam at the level it will likely be asked. The guide assumes that you have at least a rudimentary knowledge of SQL. While the guide works from basic principles of SQL, no book in and of itself is a substitute for hands-on experience. You need to have spent time writing queries, running them, and seeing the results before scheduling this exam. Since Oracle has made the Oracle XE version of its database free to download and use, there is no reason why anyone who wants to learn to use Oracle cannot get hands-on experience. XE will run under either Windows or Linux. Note that there is not currently a 12c version of XE, so you will not be able to practice features added in 12c such as the row limiting clause.

If much of the information presented in this guide is completely new to you -- then you need to supplement it with other sources of study materials to build a firm foundation of Oracle SQL knowledge. If you have a reasonable grounding in the basic concepts and are comfortable writing SQL statements of moderate complexity, then this book will supply you with the facts you need to pass the exam and improve your skills as a SQL developer. If you don't have any experience with SQL at all, the compressed format of this guide is not likely to be the best method for learning. It may provide you with the information you need to pass the test, but you're likely to have deficiencies as a SQL Developer. In that case, I would highly recommend using the materials at the companion website of this series that is discussed in the next section. They can help to improve your basic SQL skills to the point where this guide will be effective in honing the specific aspect you must be most familiar with in order to pass the exam.

# Additional Study Resources

The companion website to this series is www.oraclecertificationprep.com. The site contains many additional resources that can be used to study for this exam (and others). From the entry page of the website, click on the 'Exams' button, and then select the link for this test. The Exam Details page contains links to the following information sources:

- Applicable Oracle documentation.
- Third-party books relevant to the exam.
- White papers and articles on Oracle Learning Library on topics covered in the exam.
- Articles on the Web that may be useful for the exam.

The website will never link to unauthorized content such as brain dumps or illegal content such as copyrighted material made available without the consent of the author. I cannot guarantee the accuracy of the content links. While I have located the data and scanned it to ensure that it is relevant to the given exam, I did not write it and have not proofread it from a technical standpoint. The material on the Oracle Learning Library is almost certain to be completely accurate and most of the other links come from highly popular Oracle support websites and are created by experienced Oracle professionals.

I recommend that you use more than one source of study materials whenever you are preparing for a certification. Reading information presented from multiple different viewpoints can help to give you a more complete picture of any given topic. The links on the website can help you to do this. Fully understanding the information covered in this certification is not just valuable so that getting a passing score is more likely – it will also help you in your career. I guarantee that in the long run, any knowledge you gain while studying for this certification will provide more benefit to you than any piece of paper or line on your resume.

## Practice Questions

The guides in the Oracle Certification Prep series do not contain example questions. The format that they are designed around is not really compatible. The concise format used for the study guides means that adding a reasonable number of questions would nearly double the size of the guides themselves. However, because practice questions have been a common request from readers of my books, I have created a series of practice tests for the exams. The practice tests are available from the companion website listed in the previous section of this guide. They are not free, but the price is a fraction of that charged by other vendors for Oracle certification practice tests.

Unlike much of the material advertised online, these tests are not brain dumps. All of the tests are original content that I developed. Using these exams will not endanger your certification status with the Oracle certification program. I submit each test to the certification team after I finish developing it so that they can verify that they do not contain illicit material. These tests serve as an inexpensive means for any certification candidate that wants to determine how successful their preparation has been before scheduling the real exam.

As a purchaser of this study guide, you can use the following promotional code to get $2.00 off the purchase price of the practice exam for 1Z0-071: **071_CNSEWC**

The tests are available at the following URL:

http://oraclecertificationprep.com/apex/f?p=OCPSG:Practice_Tests

# Oracle and Structured Query Language (SQL)

## Identify the connection between an ERD and a Relational Database

An entity is a grouping of things (or a class of things) with rules or data in common. Among other possibilities, an entity might be used to represent a group of people, objects, activities, or concepts. In order to have relevance to a database, the entity must have some significance to an organization and there must be a requirement to store data about it. When implementing a database -- an entity corresponds to a table.

For Imaginary Airlines (a fictitious organization used for many examples in this guide), airports are an important element to their business. An entity that stores data about airports is therefore something that would need to be included in a database application for the organization. In the conceptual model, an entity is shown as simply a rectangle with the name of the entity either inside or sometimes just above the rectangle.

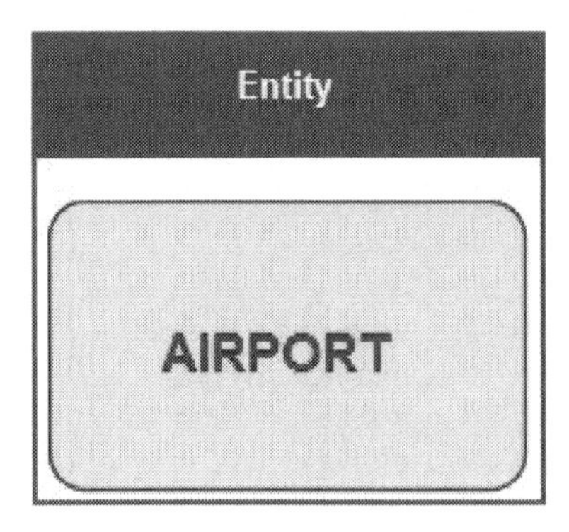


Database developers should recognize that while an entity corresponds to a table, it is not the exact same thing. An entity is an object in the real world with an independent existence. Examples of potential entities include:

- An object with physical existence (such as an airport or an aircraft).
- An object with conceptual existence (such as a flight or a ticket reservation).

Entities are the primary component of Entity Relationship Diagrams (ERDs). ERDs are used as a design aid when developing relational database applications. Below is a conceptual model ERD that contains two entities. Conceptual models are intended to show a very high-level overview of the various entities that must be contained in the database being designed and a basic idea of the relationships between entities. It does not provide specific details of the data that will be stored.

By the same token, the relationship shown between the entities has no details. In the diagram, the connecting line indicates that a relationship exists between the AIRPORT and AIRCRAFT FLEET entities, but not what the relationship is based on. If the diagram were displaying tables rather than entities, each of the tables would need to show all of the columns they contain as well as indicating which columns were acting as primary and foreign keys.

Because entities generally represent objects, their names are usually nouns. By convention, in an ERD, entity names are singular (AIRPORT rather than AIRPORTS) and they will be displayed in all capital letters (AIRPORT rather than Airport).

**Attributes**

An attribute is a piece of information that describes an entity in some fashion. They can quantify, qualify, classify, or specify the entity they belong to. In the same way that entities correspond to tables without being tables, attributes correspond to columns without actually being columns. In the conceptual diagram from the previous section, neither of the entities had attributes listed. In the Chen conceptual model ER, attributes are shown broken out from their entity as with the below diagram:

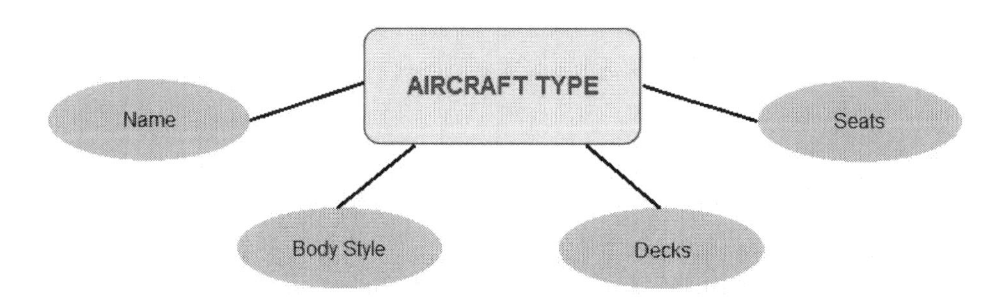


Regardless of how they are displayed in an entity relationship diagram, attributes do not provide any details about how data will be stored. Attributes will never be associated with specific data types or sizes. Attributes will be mapped to columns when the design moves to the physical model. At this point, a column must detail the type of data to be stored, the amount of space to be allocated for it, and the name that will be recorded for it in the database. For example, the 'Name' attribute in a conceptual model ERD might be a column called ACT_NAME in a physical model ERD, with a VARCHAR2 data type that is limited to 20 bytes. A physical model of the AIRCRAFT TYPE entity might look like the following image:

| AIRCRAFT_TYPES | | | |
|---|---|---|---|
| P | * | ACT_ID | NUMBER |
| | | ACT_NAME | VARCHAR2 (20 BYTE) |
| | | ACT_BODY_STYLE | VARCHAR2 (10 BYTE) |
| | | ACT_DECKS | VARCHAR2 (10 BYTE) |
| | * | ACT_SEATS | NUMBER |
| | | AIRCRAFT_TYPES_PK (ACT_ID) | |

The conceptual data model is used to help visualize the data that needs to be stored in a database and which entities are related. The physical data model documents how the data will actually be stored in the database. A physical database model will contain the table structures, including the column names, data types, and constraints. It will also include any primary keys, foreign keys, and display the relationships between each of the tables. It is possible for the physical data model to have differences from the logical data model depending on the database. While some (probably most) of the required data normalization takes place during the logical design process, it is possible that additional normalization requirements will be found during the physical design process. The diagram below shows three tables from the Imaginary Airlines schema in a logical model ERD.

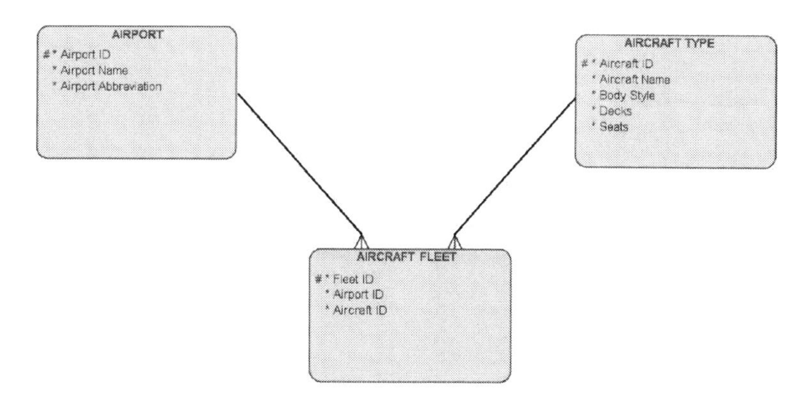

A logical model ERD is converted to a physical mode ERD using the following basic steps:

1. Convert entities into tables.
2. Convert relationships into foreign keys.
3. Convert attributes into columns.
4. Modify the physical data model based on physical constraints / requirements.

Shown below is a physical model diagram that contains the three tables from the Imaginary Airlines database that correspond to the three entities in the previous diagram. In contrast to the logical model, the columns displayed in the diagram list the data types and sizes. The column names also match what is actually stored in the database (i.e. 'ACT_BODY_STYLE') rather than a human-friendly name (i.e. 'Body Style'). The physical model also includes the primary and foreign key columns. Unlike the conceptual or logical models, the physical model is database-specific. Not all relational databases use the same data types, for example.

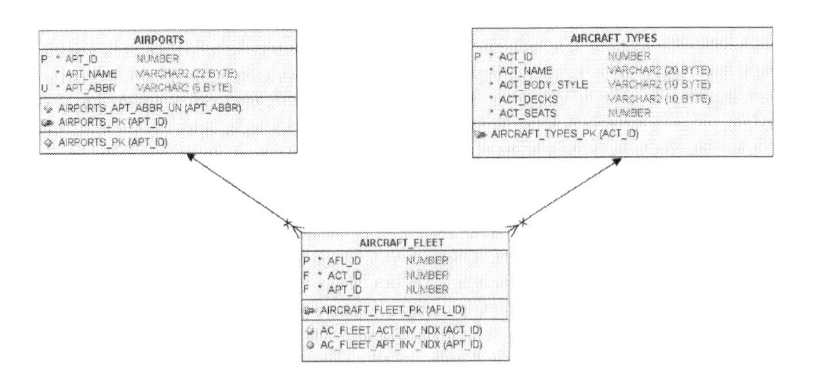


If two entities in an ERD have a relationship (for example entity A and entity B) there will always be an expectation of how many instances in A relate to how many instances in B. There are only three possibilities:

- **One-to-one** -- A single instance in A will never relate to more than a single instance in B.
- **One-to-many** -- A single instance in A can relate to one or more instances in B.
- **Many-to-many** -- Multiple instances in A can relate to multiple instances in B.

On an ER diagram, there are actually four different notations to represent the above three possibilities because the one-to-many is broken out by direction:

- **1:1** -- one-to-one
- **1:N** -- one-to-many
- **M:1** -- many-to-one
- **M:N** -- many-to-many

There are a number of different ERD notation styles that provide ways of indicating in the relationships the exact cardinality and ordinality that exists between two entities. Some of the possible options include the following:

| Left | Right | Cardinality | Example |
|---|---|---|---|
| 1 | 1 | One-to-one | Aircraft <-> Electrical System |
| 0..1 | 1 | Optional on one side one-to-one | Flight e-ticket <-> Flight Reservation |
| 0..* or * | 1..* or * | Optional on one side many-to-many | Flight Survey <-> Aircraft Flight |
| 1..* or * | 1..* or * | Many-to-many | Airline Customer <-> Aircraft Flight |
| 1 | 0..* | Optional on one side one-to-many | Airport <-> Aircraft Fleet |
| 1 | 1..* | One-to-many | Airline Customer <-> Flight Reservation |

## First, Second, and Third Normal Forms

The term 'normalization' was first used with databases by E.F. Codd, the creator of the relational model. It refers to the process of organizing the logical structure of a database in order to facilitate both ad-hoc queries and data updates. The most common term you will encounter as a database developer when dealing with normalization is 'Third Normal Form', sometimes abbreviated as 3NF. A table is in third normal form when it meets all of the following three rules:

- **First rule of normalization** -- A table shall contain no repeating groups.
- **Second rule of normalization** -- If a table has a compound primary key, and one or more fields in a table depend on only part of the primary key for that table, move them to a separate table along with that part of the key.
- **Third rule of normalization** -- If one or more fields in a table do not depend at all on the primary key for that table (or any part of it), move them to a separate table along with copies of the fields on which they do depend.

**Determinants and dependencies**

To be able to normalize entities, it is necessary to understand determinants and dependants. A determinant is any attribute (simple or composite) on which some other attribute is fully functionally dependent. The terms determinant and dependent can be described as follows:

- The expression **A → B** means 'if I know the value of A, then I can obtain the value of B.'
- In the expression **A → B**, A is the determinant and B is the dependent attribute.
- The value A determines the value of B.
- The value B depends on the value of A.

When more than one attribute acts as the determinant for an entity, it is possible for the dependent attributes to be fully or partially dependent. Given an entity for four attributes, A, B, C and D, where **AB → CD**:

- **Fully Functional Dependency** -- The entity has a fully functional dependency if both A & B are required in order to know the values of both C & D. That is to say, **AB → CD**, and **A does not→ CD** and **B does not→ CD**.

- **Partially Functional Dependency** -- The entity has a partially functional dependency if both A & B are **not** required in order to know the values of both C & D. That is to say, **AB → CD**, and any of the following are also true: **A → C** or **A → D** or **B → C** or **B → D**.

## Explain the relationship between a database and SQL

Structured Query Language, almost always referred to as SQL (pronounced either see-kwell or as separate letters: ess-kyu-ell), is a programming language that was designed for managing items held in databases. SQL was originally based upon relational algebra and tuple relational calculus. Despite not adhering entirely to the relational model as originally defined by E.F. Codd, SQL has become the most widely used database language in existence.

Although there are dialects of SQL for different database vendors, it is nevertheless the closest thing to a standard query language that currently exists. In 1986, ANSI approved a rudimentary version of SQL as the official standard. However, most vendors have included many extensions to the ANSI standard in their products. Many vendors support mostly ANSI-compliant SQL, but few (if any) are 100% compliant.

The SQL language is used by many databases to access and store data. It allows users to not only query and modify data, but also to communicate with the DBMS to add new tables or other database objects, control numerous database settings, and perform maintenance operations. While many GUIs exist that allow users to interact graphically with relational database -- at their base the interfaces are using SQL to power this interaction.

The SQL language is split into four broad categories:

- **Data Definition Language (DDL)** -- DDL statements define, structurally change, and drop schema objects in the database.
- **Data Control Language (DCL)** – DCL statements are used to control access to data stored in a database.
- **Data Manipulation Language (DML)** -- DML statements query or manipulate data in existing schema objects. DML statements do not change the structure of the database, the only query or change the contents of the database.
- **Transaction Control** -- Transaction control statements manage the changes made by DML statements and group DML statements into transactions.

SQL is the standard language used to work with relational databases and it is almost impossible to deal with one to any degree without requiring a reasonable level of familiarity with the language. SQL is used by database administrators, developers, architects, data analysts, business intelligence specialists, and more. If you do not currently know much about the language but plan to work with databases, you should make learning it a high priority. There are a number of terms and concepts that may appear throughout the next several chapters:

- **Alias** – Aliases are used to provide an alternate (usually shorter or more readable) name for an item in the select list or for a table reference. Aliases improve readability of the statement and are required for certain operations.
- **Keyword** – Keywords are defined individual elements of a SQL statement (SELECT, FROM, WHERE, GROUP BY, etc.)
- **Clause** – A clause is a subset of a SQL statement that is tied to a keyword. For example, "SELECT first_name, last_name" is a SELECT clause.
- **Expression** – An expression is an element in a select list that is not a column. It may or may not contain a column. For example, given the clause "SELECT last_name, first_name, first_name || ' ' || last_name", two elements in the clause (first_name and last_name) are columns, and (first_name || ' ' || last_name) is an expression.

- **Statement** – A statement is a combination of two or more clauses that form a complete SQL operation. At the bare minimum a SQL statement must include a SELECT clause and a FROM clause.
- **Text Literals** -- Used to specify values whenever 'string' appears in the syntax of expressions, conditions, SQL functions, and SQL statements. Text literals are always surrounded by single quotation marks.

## Describe the purpose of DDL

One of the most critical aspects of a relational database is its data dictionary. The data dictionary is a read-only set of tables that contain metadata about the database. A data dictionary contains all of the information about the database structure including:

- The definitions of every schema object in the database
- The amount of space allocated for and currently used by the schema objects
- The names of database users
- Privileges and roles granted to database users
- Auditing information

The data dictionary is a central part of how the Database Management System (DBMS) maintains and controls the system. The DBMS uses the data dictionary to perform many actions such as locating information about users, schema objects, and storage structures. Because the data dictionary data is itself stored in tables, database users can query the data using SQL. Data Definition Language (DDL) statements are used to make changes to the data dictionary. They are utilized to perform the following tasks (among others):

- Create, alter, and drop schema objects
- Analyze information on a table, index, or cluster
- Grant and revoke privileges and roles

Sometimes you will see the SQL statements that grant and revoke privileges and roles broken out of DDL into a separate category called Data Control Language (DCL). Oracle lists them under DDL, but not all vendors may do so.

Some examples of the types of objects that are acted on by DDL commands include:

- **TABLE** -- The basic structure to hold user data.
- **INDEX** -- A schema object that contains an entry for each value that appears in one or more columns of a table and provides direct, fast access to rows.
- **VIEW** -- A logical table based on one or more tables or views, although it contains no data itself.
- **CONSTRAINT** -- A rule that restricts the values in a database column.
- **USER** -- An account through which database users can log in to the database and which provides the basis for creating schema objects.

Taking users as an example database object class, there are three basic DDL commands that will operate on it:

- **CREATE USER** – Creates a new user account in the relational database.
- **ALTER USER** – Makes a change to an existing user account.
- **DROP USER** – Removes an existing user account from the database.

The same three commands (CREATE, ALTER, DROP) exist for most objects in a database

## Describe the purpose of DML

Data Manipulation Language (DML) is the name given to the SQL statements used to manage data in a relational database. DML statements include INSERT, UPDATE, DELETE and MERGE. Each of these statements manipulates data in tables.

The SELECT statement is generally grouped with the other four statements under the DML class of SQL operations. However, SELECT statements do not add, alter, or remove rows from database tables – so no manipulation is involved. However, if the SELECT command is not included with DML, then it has no place to be. It certainly does not fit in with Data Definition Language (DDL), Data Control Language (DCL), or Transaction Control Language (TCL). Just be aware that when reference is made to DML statements, the context may not include SELECT operations.

Data manipulation language statements are utilized to manage data in existing schema objects. DML statements do not modify information in the data dictionary and do not implicitly commit the current transaction. The most commonly identified DML commands are:

- **INSERT** – Used to populate data in tables. It is possible to insert one row into one table, one row into multiple tables, multiple rows into one table, or multiple rows into multiple tables.
- **UPDATE** – Used to alter data that has already been inserted into a database table. An UPDATE can affect a single row or multiple rows, and a single column or multiple columns. The WHERE clause will determine which rows in the table are altered. When executed with no WHERE clause, it will update all rows in the target table. A single UPDATE statement can only act on one table.
- **DELETE** – Used to remove previously inserted rows from a table. The command can remove a single row or multiple rows from a table. When executed with no WHERE clause, it will remove all rows from the target table. It is not possible to delete individual columns – the entire row is deleted or it is not.
- **MERGE** – Used for hybrid DML operations. The MERGE can insert, update and delete rows in a table all in a single statement. There

is no operation that a MERGE can perform that could not be performed by a combination of INSERT, UPDATE and DELETE.

## Build a SELECT statement to retrieve data from an Oracle Database table

Essentially all operations that pull data out of a table in an Oracle database have a SELECT command involved at some level. A top-level SELECT statement is also referred to as a query. If there is a second SELECT nested within the first, it is called a subquery.

When a SELECT statement retrieves information from the database, it can perform the following three types of work:

- **Selection** -- You can filter the SELECT statement to choose only the rows that you want to be returned. Without filtering, a query would return every single row in the table.
- **Projection** -- You can choose only the columns that you want to be returned by your query, or create new information through the use of expressions.
- **Joining** -- You can use the SQL JOIN operators to link two or more tables to allow you to return data that is stored in more than one table.

The following diagram illustrates a query performing both selection and projection:

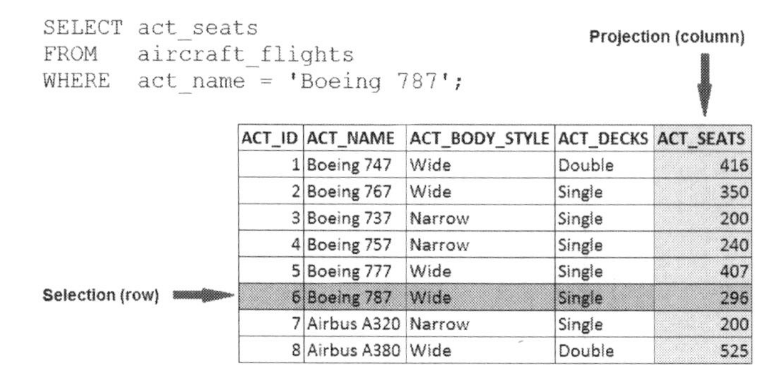

```
SELECT act_seats
FROM   aircraft_flights
WHERE  act_name = 'Boeing 787';
```

| ACT_ID | ACT_NAME | ACT_BODY_STYLE | ACT_DECKS | ACT_SEATS |
|---|---|---|---|---|
| 1 | Boeing 747 | Wide | Double | 416 |
| 2 | Boeing 767 | Wide | Single | 350 |
| 3 | Boeing 737 | Narrow | Single | 200 |
| 4 | Boeing 757 | Narrow | Single | 240 |
| 5 | Boeing 777 | Wide | Single | 407 |
| 6 | Boeing 787 | Wide | Single | 296 |
| 7 | Airbus A320 | Narrow | Single | 200 |
| 8 | Airbus A380 | Wide | Double | 525 |

The syntax of a minimal SELECT statement in Oracle is:

```
SELECT select_list
FROM   table_reference;
```

The four elements above (SELECT and FROM keywords and the select_list and table_reference clauses) exist in every SQL query issued to Oracle (or at least every one that completes without an error). The elements that make up the **select_list** might be columns, functions, literals, etc. The **table_reference** might be an Oracle table, remote table, external table, view, pipelined function, etc. Regardless of the specifics, they must be valid references and be present in the SELECT statement in order for it to execute successfully.

The most basic SELECT statement consists of the SELECT keyword, a list of one or more columns or expressions (the select_list noted above), the FROM keyword, and a table or view (the table_reference value shown above). When executed with only the SELECT and FROM keywords, Oracle will return all rows that currently exist in the table and the order that the rows will be returned in is indeterminate (which is to say the order is not only unpredictable but may change from one execution to the next).

```
SELECT apt_id, apt_name, apt_abbr
FROM   airports;

APT_ID APT_NAME                       APT_ABBR
------ ------------------------------ --------
     1 Orlando, FL                    MCO
     2 Atlanta, GA                    ATL
     3 Miami, FL                      MIA
     4 Jacksonville, FL               JAX
     5 Dallas/Fort Worth              DFW
```

If you wish to display all columns from a table, rather than entering each column into the SELECT clause, you can use the asterisk wildcard. The asterisk will return the complete set of columns from the table (or tables) listed in the FROM clause. If a query contains multiple tables, you can prefix the asterisk with a table name or table alias to return all columns from just one of the tables in the query.

When the asterisk is used in a SELECT, the columns to be returned by the SELECT operation are pulled directly from the data dictionary table that is used to store column information for user tables. The columns in the SELECT list will appear in the order that they are stored in that table and cannot be altered. The column headings returned by the operation will be the upper-case column names as stored in the data dictionary. There is no way to use the asterisk *and* supply column aliases or change the column order.

```
SELECT *
FROM   airports;

APT_ID APT_NAME                       APT_ABBR
------ ------------------------------ --------
     1 Orlando, FL                    MCO
     2 Atlanta, GA                    ATL
     3 Miami, FL                      MIA
     4 Jacksonville, FL               JAX
     5 Dallas/Fort Worth              DFW
```

In the below example, the query contains two tables joined together. The asterisk used in the SELECT list returns all columns from both tables. Both tables contain a column called APT_ID (which is how the two are joined) and so that column is returned once for each table.

```
SELECT *
FROM   airports apt
       INNER JOIN aircraft_fleet afl
       ON apt.apt_id = afl.apt_id;

APT_ID APT_NAME               APT_ABBR AFL_ID ACT_ID APT_ID
------ ---------------------- -------- ------ ------ ------
     1 Orlando, FL            MCO           1      2      1
     1 Orlando, FL            MCO           2      2      1
     2 Atlanta, GA            ATL           3      3      2
     2 Atlanta, GA            ATL           4      4      2
     3 Miami, FL              MIA           5      1      3
     3 Miami, FL              MIA           6      1      3
     5 Dallas/Fort Worth      DFW           7      1      5
     5 Dallas/Fort Worth      DFW           8      2      5
```

When the asterisk is prefixed with the AIRPORTS table alias, only the columns from that table are returned:

```
SELECT apt.*
FROM   airports apt
       INNER JOIN aircraft_fleet afl
       ON apt.apt_id = afl.apt_id;

APT_ID APT_NAME               APT_ABBR
------ ---------------------- --------
     1 Orlando, FL            MCO
     1 Orlando, FL            MCO
     2 Atlanta, GA            ATL
     2 Atlanta, GA            ATL
     3 Miami, FL              MIA
     3 Miami, FL              MIA
     5 Dallas/Fort Worth      DFW
     5 Dallas/Fort Worth      DFW
```

In order to return a subset of the columns in the two tables and control the order of display, it is necessary to supply the columns to be returned:

```
SELECT APT_ABBR, APT_NAME, ACT_ID
FROM   airports apt
       INNER JOIN aircraft_fleet afl
       ON apt.apt_id = afl.apt_id;

APT_ABBR APT_NAME                   ACT_ID
-------- ---------------------- ----------
MCO      Orlando, FL                     2
MCO      Orlando, FL                     2
ATL      Atlanta, GA                     3
ATL      Atlanta, GA                     4
MIA      Miami, FL                       1
MIA      Miami, FL                       1
DFW      Dallas/Fort Worth               1
DFW      Dallas/Fort Worth               2
```

**Lexical Conventions**

The Oracle SQL parser treats single spaces, multiple spaces, and tabs interchangeably. That is to say it doesn't matter when writing SQL if you use one space or fifty, or a tab instead of a space. A single carriage return can be used in lieu of a space in most cases. Two carriage returns together signal the end of a SQL statement. The following SQL statements would be treated identically by the Oracle SQL Parser:

```
SELECT emp_last,emp_first,salary/2080 FROM employees
WHERE emp_job='Pilot' ORDER BY salary;

SELECT emp_last, emp_first, salary / 2080
FROM   employees
WHERE  emp_job = 'Pilot'
ORDER BY salary;

SELECT emp_last,
       emp_first,
       salary / 2080
FROM   employees
WHERE  emp_job = 'Pilot'
ORDER BY salary;

SELECT
emp_last,
emp_first,
salary / 2080
FROM
employees
WHERE
emp_job = 'Pilot'
ORDER BY
salary;
```

SQL Statements are not case-sensitive with the exception of quoted elements. The following statement is equivalent to the ones above. Changing the case of the quoted element 'Pilot', however, would alter the results of the SQL statement. Note that SINGLE quotes are used to enclose character literals in SQL statements. DOUBLE quotes in SQL statements are used to enclose names used by the Oracle SQL parser (column names, column aliases, table names, table aliases, etc.)

```
select EMP_LAST, EMP_FIRST, SALARY / 2080
from   EMPLOYEES
where  EMP_JOB = 'Pilot'
order by SALARY;
```

Keywords cannot be split across lines, abbreviated, or run together with the rest of their clause without a separator. The separation can be a space, tab, or carriage return, but it must be present. The following three statements would generate an error for each of the three reasons supplied above respectively.

```
SELECT emp_last, emp_first, salary/2080
FROM   employees
WHERE  emp_job='Pilot' ORD
ER BY     salary;

SEL    emp_last, emp_first, salary/2080
FRM    employees
WHR    emp_job='Pilot'
ORD BY salary;

SELECTemp_last,emp_first,salary/2080FROMemployees
WHEREemp_job='Pilot'ORDER BYsalary;
```

It should be noted that you can split multi-word keywords with a carriage return, although it would be a very bad practice to actually do so. The following statement will execute successfully, but **please** do not write code like this on the job.

```
SELECT emp_last,
       emp_first,
       salary / 2080
FROM   employees
WHERE  emp_job = 'Pilot'
ORDER
BY salary;
```

SQL Statements that will be persistent (i.e. part of a script or procedure as opposed to a single-use ad-hoc query), should be formatted for readability. The use of indentation and selective capitalization will make SQL statements, especially large and complex ones, much easier to read and maintain. Spending a few extra seconds making your SQL readable will result in bigger time savings if you ever have to look back at your work in the future.

This may seem like a small thing, but it has career implications. Not all experienced developers write well-formatted code. However, enough do that it is one element I use in evaluating potential new hires. Even if someone is very knowledgeable of SQL, but creates poorly formatted code, this is a significant downside. In most environments multiple developers work together and must be able to easily interpret code developed by the other team members. When the SQL is sloppy this is made more difficult than it should be.

## Arithmetic Operators & Precedence

Arithmetic operators can be used with one or two arguments to add, subtract, multiply, and divide numeric values. The addition and subtraction operators can also be used in datetime and interval arithmetic. The arguments used must resolve to numeric data types or to a data type that can be implicitly converted to a numeric type (datetime data types meet this requirement because they are stored internally by Oracle as a numeric value).

You can perform math operations directly via a SQL statement:

```
SELECT 4+4
FROM   dual;

4+4
---
  8
```

You can also use arithmetic operators to modify the results returned from data in a table:

```
SELECT emp_last, emp_first, salary, salary * 1.05 SAL_WITH_RAISE
FROM   employees
WHERE  emp_job = 'Pilot'
ORDER BY salary DESC;
```

```
EMP_LAST   EMP_FIRST  SALARY SAL_WITH_RAISE
---------- ---------- ------ --------------
McCoy      Phil       105000         110250
Thomas     James       98500         103425
Jones      John        97500         102375
Kia        Noh         92250        96862.5
Gun        Top         91500          96075
Skytalker  Luke        90000          94500
Aptop      Dell        87500          91875
Picard     John        49500          51975
```

Likewise date literals can be manipulated directly via SQL using arithmetic operators, or date values in a table altered:

```
SELECT SYSDATE, SYSDATE+5
FROM   dual;

SYSDATE   SYSDATE+5
--------- ---------
10-AUG-13 15-AUG-13


SELECT emp_last, emp_first, start_date, start_date + 60
FROM   employees
WHERE  emp_job = 'Pilot'
ORDER BY start_date;

EMP_LAST   EMP_FIRST  START_DATE START_DATE+60
---------- ---------- ---------- -------------
Jones      John       10-APR-95  09-JUN-95
McCoy      Phil       09-JUN-96  08-AUG-96
Gun        Top        13-OCT-96  12-DEC-96
Thomas     James      12-MAY-99  11-JUL-99
Picard     John       11-NOV-01  10-JAN-02
Skytalker  Luke       10-SEP-02  09-NOV-02
Aptop      Dell       22-AUG-03  21-OCT-03
Kia        Noh        07-JUL-04  05-SEP-04
```

Precedence is what determines the order in which different operators in the same expression are evaluated. Oracle evaluates operators with higher precedence before evaluating those with lower precedence. If there are operators with equal precedence, they are evaluated from left to right within the expression. The plus and minus signs have two different levels of precedence depending on their usage. Both can be used in either a unary fashion or in a binary fashion depending on whether they are applied to one or two operands. For example, in '-1', the negative sign is acting as a unary operator and evaluates to 'negative one'. By contrast, in '4 - 1' the negative sign is acting as a binary operator and evaluates to 'four minus one'. The arithmetic operators and their precedence follow:

1. **+, - (as unary operators)** -- Identity, negation,
2. ***, /** -- Multiplication, division
3. **+, - (as binary operators)** -- Addition, subtraction

In the below example, the multiplication symbol has a higher precedence than the plus sign. Oracle multiplies two times four and then adds three to the result:

```
SELECT 3 + 2 * 4
FROM   dual;

3+2*4
-----
   11
```

Parentheses can be used to change the order in which the operators are evaluated. When parentheses are nested, the most deeply nested operators are evaluated first. In the following example, the operation is three plus two and then the result is multiplied by four.

```
SELECT (3 + 2) * 4
FROM   dual;

(3+2)*4
-------
     20
```

When the negative sign is used as a unary operator, it takes precedence over multiplication or division:

```
SELECT -2 * 6
FROM   dual;

-2*6
----
 -12
```

## Column Aliases

The default heading returned for columns selected in a query is simply the column name itself. If the SELECT list item is an expression, the text of the expression with spaces removed is returned. For a SELECT it may be desirable to provide a cleaner, shorter, or more descriptive heading for the results. For some SQL operations, providing an alias for expressions is a requirement. To specify an alias for a column or expression, you can provide the alias immediately after the column name, separated by a space. You can also use the optional 'AS' keyword when specifying an alias. The AS keyword makes the resulting query more readable, especially for long statements. By default, aliases are returned in upper-case and cannot have spaces or special characters. You can bypass that restriction by enclosing the alias in double-quotation marks. The four examples below show the same SQL statement using no alias, two alternate syntaxes for aliasing columns and the use of an alias enclosed by double quotes.

```
SELECT emp_first, emp_last,
       emp_first || ' ' || emp_last
FROM   employees
WHERE  emp_job = 'CEO';

EMP_FIRST  EMP_LAST   EMP_FIRST||''||EMP_LAST
---------- ---------- -----------------------
Big        Boss       Big Boss

SELECT emp_first, emp_last,
       emp_first || ' ' || emp_last full_name
FROM   employees
WHERE  emp_job = 'CEO';

EMP_FIRST  EMP_LAST   FULL_NAME
---------- ---------- ---------------------
Big        Boss       Big Boss
```

```
SELECT emp_first, emp_last,
       emp_first || ' ' || emp_last AS full_name
FROM   employees
WHERE  emp_job = 'CEO';

EMP_FIRST  EMP_LAST   FULL_NAME
---------- ---------- ---------------------
Big        Boss       Big Boss
```

```
SELECT emp_first, emp_last,
       emp_first || ' ' || emp_last AS "Full Name"
FROM   employees
WHERE  emp_job = 'CEO';

EMP_FIRST  EMP_LAST   Full Name
---------- ---------- ---------------------
Big        Boss       Big Boss
```

## Expressions

Expressions in the select list of a SQL statement include essentially everything except a bare column name. They could be literals, column data that has been modified by operators, or SQL functions.

- **Text Literals** -- Use to specify values whenever 'string' appears in the syntax of expressions, conditions, SQL functions, and SQL statements. Text literals are always surrounded by single quotation marks.

```
SELECT 'Fred' AS STRING_LIT
FROM   dual;

STRING_LIT
----------
Fred
```

Text literals can be combined with information being selected from a table in order to provide context or formatting.

```
SELECT emp_last || ', ' || emp_first || ' (' || emp_job ||
       ') started on ' || start_date AS EMP_BIO
FROM   employees
WHERE  emp_job = 'Pilot';

EMP_BIO
-------------------------------------------------
Jones, John (Pilot) started on 10-APR-95
Gun, Top (Pilot) started on 13-OCT-96
McCoy, Phil (Pilot) started on 09-JUN-96
Thomas, James (Pilot) started on 12-MAY-99
Picard, John (Pilot) started on 11-NOV-01
Skytalker, Luke (Pilot) started on 10-SEP-02
Aptop, Dell (Pilot) started on 22-AUG-03
Kia, Noh (Pilot) started on 07-JUL-04
```

- **Numeric Literals** -- Use numeric literal notation to specify fixed and floating-point numbers.

```
SELECT 14.5 AS NUM_LIT
FROM   dual;

NUM_LIT
-------
14.5
```

- **Datetime Literals** -- You can specify a date value as a string literal, or you can convert a character or numeric value to a date value using the TO_DATE function.

```
SELECT '10-JAN-16' AS STRING_LIT,
       TO_DATE('01/10/2016', 'MM/DD/YYYY') AS TD_LIT
FROM   dual;

STRING_LIT TD_LIT
---------- ---------
10-JAN-16  10-JAN-16
```

In the above statement, the second column was explicitly converted to a date data type, but the value returned by SQL*Plus looks exactly like the string in the first column. This is because Oracle does not ever display dates as they are stored in the database. What Oracle actually stores in a DATE field behind the scenes is a numeric value. Internally, dates in Oracle are stored as a fixed-length, seven-byte field. The information in the seven bytes is:

1. The Century
2. The Year
3. The Month
4. The Day
5. The Hour
6. The Minute
7. The Second

If this information were displayed as it is stored, the result would not make sense from a human standpoint. Because of this, whenever a data is displayed as the result of a SELECT operation, Oracle automatically converts it to a character value. The default date format for this is dependent on how the database was created and the value chosen for the NLS_DATE_FORMAT initialization parameter. The most common format for databases created in the US is 'DD-MON-YY'. It is possible to alter the default by setting the NLS_DATE_FORMAT parameter at the system of session level. Individual SELECT statements can return specific formats by making use of the TO_CHAR parameter and providing a format model.

# Restricting and Sorting Data

## Use the ORDER BY clause to sort SQL query results

The ORDER BY clause of a SQL query allows you to determine the sort order of the rows returned by the operation. When a SQL statement does not contain an ORDER BY clause, the order of the rows being returned is indeterminate. Often rows will be returned in the order they were inserted into a table, but that is not always the case. The same query may not return rows in the same order in all cases. If the order is important, then you should use the ORDER BY clause even if you find that the rows return in the order you want without the clause (because the order might change at some future date). When the ORDER BY clause is used, it must always be the last clause of the SQL statement. When a SQL statement has subqueries, it is possible to use an ORDER BY clause for them, but generally pointless. The final ORDER BY determines the sort order of the data returned to the user. It is not possible to use LONG or LOB columns in an ORDER BY clause.

```
SELECT NAME, STYLE, DECKS, SEATS
FROM
(
SELECT ACT_NAME       AS NAME,
       ACT_BODY_STYLE AS STYLE,
       ACT_DECKS      AS DECKS,
       ACT_SEATS      AS SEATS
FROM   aircraft_types
ORDER BY act_seats
)
WHERE  decks = 'Single'
ORDER BY name;

NAME         STYLE      DECKS      SEATS
------------ ---------- ---------- -----
Boeing 737   Narrow     Single       200
Boeing 757   Narrow     Single       240
Boeing 767   Wide       Single       350
```

It's possible to sort by a single column or by multiple columns (or expressions). When sorting by multiple columns, the precedence of the sort order will be determined by the position of the expression in the ORDER BY clause. The leftmost expression will provide the initial sort order and each expression to the right will be evaluated in turn. By default, data is sorted in ascending order (1-2-3-4 / a-b-c-d). One item of note is the fact that upper and lower case characters don't sort together. When Oracle sorts by character values, it is actually using the ASCII values for the logic. Because of this, a lower case 'a' will sort *higher* than an upper case 'Z'. In addition, numeric data in a character field does not sort as you would expect. For example, if you were to sort table rows with values containing '1', '2', and '100' in ascending order, the result would be 1-100-2. To sort number data in a character field in numeric order, you would have to use the TO_NUMBER function against the column in the ORDER BY clause to convert the data for sort purposes. That said, if the column contains non-numeric data in addition to the numeric data, using TO_NUMBER will generate an error if it hits one of those rows.

```
SELECT char_column
FROM   sort_example
ORDER BY char_column;

CHAR_COLUMN
-----------
1
100
2
A
B
C
a
b
c
```

The SORT_EXAMPLE table has a NUMBER column as well. When a query is sorted by it, the expected 'numeric' sort results are returned.

```
SELECT num_column
FROM   sort_example
ORDER BY num_column;
```

```
NUM_COLUMN
----------
         1
         2
         3
        10
        20
        30
       100
       200
       300
```

If the data is sorted by the column after being converted to character data, the result is completely different:

```
SELECT num_column
FROM   sort_example
ORDER BY TO_CHAR(num_column);

NUM_COLUMN
----------
         1
        10
       100
         2
        20
       200
         3
        30
       300
```

By default NULLS are sorted last when a sort is in ascending order and first when descending. Effectively when being sorted, NULLs are treated as an infinitely high value. The default behavior can be reversed by adding NULLS LAST when sorting in descending order or NULLS FIRST when sorting in ascending order.

```
SELECT *
FROM   aircraft_fleet
ORDER BY apt_id;
```

```
AFL_ID ACT_ID APT_ID
------ ------ ------
     1      2      1
     2      2      1
     3      3      2
     4      4      2
     5      1      3
     6      1      3
     7      1      5
     8      2      5
     9      4
    10      3
```

```
SELECT *
FROM   aircraft_fleet
ORDER BY apt_id NULLS FIRST;
```

```
AFL_ID ACT_ID APT_ID
------ ------ ------
     9      4
    10      3
     2      2      1
     1      2      1
     3      3      2
     4      4      2
     6      1      3
     5      1      3
     7      1      5
     8      2      5
```

When specifying the expressions to sort by, you can use either the expression itself, the alias for the expression, or the numeric value of its position in the SELECT list. Using the position rather than the expression can be useful of the expression being sorted on is complex. It is also useful when sorting compound queries using the set operators (UNION, INTERSECT, MINUS) where the column names may not match. Set operators will be discussed in a later section.

```
SELECT APT_ID, APT_NAME, APT_ABBR
FROM   airports
ORDER BY apt_name;
```

```
APT_ID APT_NAME                       APT_ABBR
------ ------------------------------ --------
     2 Atlanta, GA                    ATL
     5 Dallas/Fort Worth              DFW
     4 Jacksonville, FL               JAX
     3 Miami, FL                      MIA
     1 Orlando, FL                    MCO
```

```
SELECT *
FROM   airports
ORDER BY 2;

APT_ID APT_NAME                       APT_ABBR
------ ------------------------------ --------
     2 Atlanta, GA                    ATL
     5 Dallas/Fort Worth              DFW
     4 Jacksonville, FL               JAX
     3 Miami, FL                      MIA
     1 Orlando, FL                    MCO
```

To reverse the sort order of columns, you can use the descending operator, DESC.

```
SELECT *
FROM   airports
ORDER BY 2 DESC;

APT_ID APT_NAME               APT_ABBR
------ ---------------------- --------
     1 Orlando, FL            MCO
     3 Miami, FL              MIA
     4 Jacksonville, FL       JAX
     5 Dallas/Fort Worth      DFW
     2 Atlanta, GA            ATL
```

The default sort order on columns is always ascending. If a column is sorted on more than one column, and you want to change multiple columns to sort in descending order, each would need its own DESC keyword. The following query sorts by three columns. First it sorts all the rows by the EMP_JOB field in ascending order. For all employees in the same job, it sorts rows by the AIRCRAFT_TYPE in descending order. For all rows with the same job and aircraft type, it sorts in ascending order by last name.

```
SELECT emp_job,
        (SELECT act_name
         FROM   aircraft_types act
                NATURAL JOIN aircraft_fleet afl
         WHERE  afl.afl_id = e1.afl_id) AS aircraft_type,
        emp_last,
       (SELECT emp_last
        FROM employees e2
        WHERE e2.emp_id = e1.emp_supervisor) AS MANAGER
FROM   employees e1
ORDER BY emp_job, aircraft_type DESC, emp_last;

EMP_JOB    AIRCRAFT_TYPE EMP_LAST   MANAGER
---------- ------------- ---------- ----------
CEO                      Boss
CFO                      Smith      Boss
Mgr                      Storm      Alien
Pilot      Boeing 767    Gun        Storm
Pilot      Boeing 767    Jones      Storm
Pilot      Boeing 767    Kia        Storm
Pilot      Boeing 757    Thomas     Storm
Pilot      Boeing 747    Aptop      Storm
Pilot      Boeing 747    Picard     Storm
Pilot      Boeing 747    Skytalker  Storm
Pilot      Boeing 737    McCoy      Storm
SVP                      Jameson    Boss
SVP                      Stoner     Boss
SrDir                    Alien      Jeckson
SrDir                    Stoneflint Abong
VP                       Abong      Jameson
VP                       Jeckson    Stoner
```

Unlike the WHERE clause, aliases can be used in the ORDER BY clause. The reason for this is because the SQL engine evaluates the WHERE clause before the select list but the ORDER BY clause after the select list.

```
SELECT APT_ID,
       APT_NAME AS AIRPORT_NAME,
       APT_ABBR AS ABBREV
FROM   airports
ORDER BY airport_name;

APT_ID AIRPORT_NAME           ABBREV
------ ---------------------- ------
     2 Atlanta, GA            ATL
     5 Dallas/Fort Worth      DFW
     4 Jacksonville, FL       JAX
     3 Miami, FL              MIA
     1 Orlando, FL            MCO
```

## Limit the rows that are retrieved by a query

The ability to retrieve specific information from a database is possibly the most important aspect of SQL. Limiting the rows being returned and defining the order they should be returned in are both significant parts of that functionality.

### DISTINCT | UNIQUE

One of the ways in which to limit the amount of data returned by a query is to display only one result when the table(s) being queried have multiple copies of duplicate data. This can be done using either the DISTINCT or UNIQUE keywords. The DISTINCT keyword is much more commonly used than the UNIQUE keyword, but either will perform the same function. When a row contains matching values for **every** expression in the select list, the DISTINCT/UNIQUE keyword will only return a single row. It is not possible to use DISTINCT/UNIQUE if one or more of the expressions being returned is a LOB column. The two statements below show the effect of adding the DISTINCT keyword to a query.

```
SELECT act_body_style, act_decks
FROM   aircraft_types;

ACT_BODY_STYLE ACT_DECKS
-------------- ----------
Wide           Double
Wide           Single
Narrow         Single
Narrow         Single


SELECT DISTINCT act_body_style, act_decks
FROM   aircraft_types;

ACT_BODY_STYLE ACT_DECKS
-------------- ----------
Wide           Single
Wide           Double
Narrow         Single
```

In the second example, the duplicated rows from the first query with a body style of narrow and a single deck have been reduced to a single row. The DISTINCT query still has two rows with a wide body style and two rows with a single deck, but no rows where every column value is identical.

The functionality works equally well when applied to a query involving multiple tables. The following example uses the UNIQUE keyword against the aliased wildcard query from the previous section and gets a result of four rows rather than the eight returned above.

```
SELECT UNIQUE apt.*
FROM   airports apt
       INNER JOIN aircraft_fleet afl
       ON apt.apt_id = afl.apt_id;

APT_ID APT_NAME               APT_ABBR
------ ---------------------- --------
     2 Atlanta, GA            ATL
     5 Dallas/Fort Worth      DFW
     1 Orlando, FL            MCO
     3 Miami, FL              MIA
```

**WHERE Clause**

The WHERE clause of SQL statements allows you to create conditions that rows must meet in order to be returned by the query. The conditions in the clause may be extremely simple or mind-numbingly complex. If you omit the WHERE clause, all rows of the table or tables in the query will be returned by the SQL (although the use of DISTINCT/UNIQUE would cause only the unique results to be displayed).

When comparing values, there are some rules that you must be aware of:

- When text or date literals are included in the where clause, they must be enclosed in single quotes.
- When a text literal is being compared to a text column, the comparison is always case-specific.

- If a date literal is being compared to a date data type in a table, Oracle must convert the literal to a DATE data type before evaluating the two. If the string value is supplied in the same format as the NLS_DATE_FORMAT for the session, then Oracle can convert the string to a date automatically. If the text does not match the NLS_DATE_FORMAT, you must use explicitly convert the value to the date data type. Date and character conversions will be covered later in this guide.

The most common comparison operators for a WHERE clause are:

- **=** -- Equal to
- **<** -- Less than
- **>** -- Greater than
- **<=** -- Less than or equal to
- **>=** -- Greater than or equal to
- **<>** -- Greater than or Less than
- **!=, ^=** -- Not equal to
- **IN(set)** – Value contained within set
- **BETWEEN val1 AND val2** – Between val1 and val2 (inclusive)
- **LIKE** – Matches a given pattern that can include wildcards
- **IS NULL** – Is a NULL value
- **IS NOT NULL** – Is a non-NULL value

The equality operator is almost assuredly the most common condition applied to filter the data being returned from a SQL query. In the example below the query will return only those rows of the AIRCRAFT_TYPES table where the ACT_DECKS is equal to the text 'Single'.

```
SELECT *
FROM   aircraft_types
WHERE  act_decks = 'Single';

ACT_ID ACT_NAME     ACT_BODY_STYLE ACT_DECKS  ACT_SEATS
------ ------------ -------------- ---------- ---------
     2 Boeing 767   Wide           Single           350
     3 Boeing 737   Narrow         Single           200
     4 Boeing 757   Narrow         Single           240
```

The results of the above query can be completely reversed by using the not-equals operator '!='. This operator (or the alternate 'not equal' operator '^=') is interchangeable with the Greater than/Less than operator '<>'.

```
SELECT *
FROM   aircraft_types
WHERE  act_decks != 'Single';

ACT_ID ACT_NAME     ACT_BODY_STYLE ACT_DECKS  ACT_SEATS
------ ------------ -------------- ---------- ---------
     1 Boeing 747   Wide           Double           416
```

The example below makes use of the less-than sign '<' for filtering the results:

```
SELECT *
FROM   aircraft_types
WHERE  act_seats < 416;

ACT_ID ACT_NAME     ACT_BODY_STYLE ACT_DECKS  ACT_SEATS
------ ------------ -------------- ---------- ---------
     2 Boeing 767   Wide           Single           350
     3 Boeing 737   Narrow         Single           200
     4 Boeing 757   Narrow         Single           240
```

The example below makes use of the IN operator for filtering the results:

```
SELECT *
FROM   aircraft_types
WHERE  act_name IN ('Boeing 737', 'Boeing 767');

ACT_ID ACT_NAME     ACT_BODY_STYLE ACT_DECKS  ACT_SEATS
------ ------------ -------------- ---------- ---------
     2 Boeing 767   Wide           Single           350
     3 Boeing 737   Narrow         Single           200
```

The example below makes use of the BETWEEN operator for filtering the results. Note that the BETWEEN is inclusive because the endpoints of 200 and 240 are included in the results. If the BETWEEN operator were NOT inclusive, the range would need to have been 199 -> 241.

```
SELECT *
FROM   aircraft_types
WHERE  act_seats BETWEEN 200
                     AND 240;

ACT_ID ACT_NAME     ACT_BODY_STYLE ACT_DECKS  ACT_SEATS
------ ------------ -------------- ---------- ---------
     3 Boeing 737   Narrow         Single           200
     4 Boeing 757   Narrow         Single           240
```

The example below shows pattern matching using the LIKE operator. The % wildcard looks for zero or more occurrences of any character or combination of characters, whereas the _ wildcard looks for a single indeterminate character. The condition below then will return any aircraft where the number '5' is the second-to-last character in the string.

```
SELECT *
FROM   aircraft_types
WHERE  act_name LIKE '%5_';

ACT_ID ACT_NAME     ACT_BODY_STYLE ACT_DECKS  ACT_SEATS
------ ------------ -------------- ---------- ---------
     4 Boeing 757   Narrow         Single           240
```

If columns are aliased in the SELECT clause, the alias names cannot be used to reference columns in the WHERE clause. When the Oracle SQL engine parses the SQL, the WHERE clause gets evaluated before the aliases are applied, so the engine does not recognize the alias.

```
SELECT ACT_NAME       AS NAME,
       ACT_BODY_STYLE AS STYLE,
       ACT_DECKS      AS DECKS,
       ACT_SEATS      AS SEATS
FROM   aircraft_types
WHERE  decks = 'Single';

SQL Error: ORA-00904: "DECKS": invalid identifier
00904. 00000 -  "%s: invalid identifier"
*Cause:
*Action:
```

The following example is able to make use of the 'DECKS' alias in the WHERE clause, however. This is because the aliased columns are inside of parenthesis and the WHERE clause is outside. Just as with the earlier discussion on operators, the Oracle SQL engine will evaluate SQL text inside of parenthesis prior to SQL outside of it. By the time the WHERE clause is evaluated, the aliases have already been applied to the columns.

```
SELECT NAME, STYLE, DECKS, SEATS
FROM
(
SELECT ACT_NAME       AS NAME,
       ACT_BODY_STYLE AS STYLE,
       ACT_DECKS      AS DECKS,
       ACT_SEATS      AS SEATS
FROM   aircraft_types
)
WHERE  decks = 'Single';

NAME         STYLE      DECKS      SEATS
------------ ---------- ---------- -----
Boeing 767   Wide       Single       350
Boeing 737   Narrow     Single       200
Boeing 757   Narrow     Single       240
```

**Combining two or more conditions with Logical Operators**

There are three logical operators that can be used in conjunction with operators in a WHERE clause to generate more complex (and specific) logic for identifying rows:

- **AND** – Evaluates to TRUE if the components on both sides are TRUE.
- **OR** -- Evaluates to TRUE if the component on either side are TRUE.
- **NOT** – Evaluates to TRUE if the identified component is FALSE

When two or more conditions in a WHERE clause are combined (or reversed) through the use of logical operators, results are returned by the query only when the complete clause evaluates to TRUE. The following two examples make use of two conditions each, the first combined with the 'AND' operator and the second with the 'OR' operator. In the first statement, both conditions have to evaluate to TRUE for a row to be returned. In the second, a row is returned if either condition evaluates to TRUE.

```
SELECT *
FROM   aircraft_types
WHERE  act_seats < 416
AND    act_body_style = 'Narrow';

ACT_ID ACT_NAME     ACT_BODY_STYLE ACT_DECKS  ACT_SEATS
------ ------------ -------------- ---------- ---------
     3 Boeing 737   Narrow         Single           200
     4 Boeing 757   Narrow         Single           240
```

```
SELECT *
FROM   aircraft_types
WHERE  act_seats < 220
OR     act_decks = 'Double';

ACT_ID ACT_NAME     ACT_BODY_STYLE ACT_DECKS  ACT_SEATS
------ ------------ -------------- ---------- ---------
     1 Boeing 747   Wide           Double           416
     3 Boeing 737   Narrow         Single           200
```

If a WHERE clause contains a combination of both 'AND' and 'OR' operators, it is very likely that the conditions must be combined within parentheses for the desired results to be achieved. In the below example, the first condition excludes planes with more than one deck (the 747). This is AND'ed with the second condition that filters out planes with a wide body style deck (excluding the 747 and 767). The final condition is OR'd in and provides an exception for planes with more than 200 seats.

The intent of the final condition is to include the 767 but exclude the 747 (the logic being to have one deck and either a narrow body or greater than 200 seats). However, the result of the query has all four aircraft types. The reason for this is that the OR operator has equal precedence with the AND operator. The clause as written will return planes with either of the following conditions:

- A single deck and not a wide body style
- Greater than 200 seats

```
SELECT *
FROM   aircraft_types
WHERE  act_decks = 'Single'
AND    act_body_style != 'Wide'
OR     act_seats > 200;

ACT_ID ACT_NAME     ACT_BODY_STYLE ACT_DECKS  ACT_SEATS
------ ------------ -------------- ---------- ---------
     1 Boeing 747   Wide           Double           416
     2 Boeing 767   Wide           Single           350
     3 Boeing 737   Narrow         Single           200
     4 Boeing 757   Narrow         Single           240
```

To return the 767 and not the 747, the second and third conditions must be evaluated together and then the result ANDed to the first condition. To do this, the conditions must be enclosed by parentheses to change the order of evaluation. The updated clause will return planes with both of the following conditions:

- A single deck.
- Greater than 200 seats and not a wide body style.

```
SELECT *
FROM   aircraft_types
WHERE  act_decks = 'Single'
AND    (     act_body_style != 'Wide'
         OR  act_seats > 200);

ACT_ID ACT_NAME     ACT_BODY_STYLE ACT_DECKS  ACT_SEATS
------ ------------ -------------- ---------- ---------
     2 Boeing 767   Wide           Single           350
     3 Boeing 737   Narrow         Single           200
     4 Boeing 757   Narrow         Single           240
```

Changing the order of the conditions in the SELECT statement would also have altered the results. The better option is the parentheses, however. Parentheses make it clear from the outset which conditions are intended to be evaluated together.

```
SELECT *
FROM   aircraft_types
WHERE  act_body_style != 'Wide'
OR     act_seats > 200
AND    act_decks = 'Single';

ACT_ID ACT_NAME     ACT_BODY_STYLE ACT_DECKS  ACT_SEATS
------ ------------ -------------- ---------- ---------
     2 Boeing 767   Wide           Single           350
     3 Boeing 737   Narrow         Single           200
     4 Boeing 757   Narrow         Single           240
```

The NOT logical operator reverses a given operator. The statement below has the condition 'WHERE NOT act_decks = 'Single'. This could just as easily be written 'WHERE act_decks != 'Single'. However, NOT is the only practical way to reverse the BETWEEN, IN, IS NULL, or LIKE operators.

```
SELECT *
FROM   aircraft_types
WHERE  NOT act_decks = 'Single';

ACT_ID ACT_NAME     ACT_BODY_STYLE ACT_DECKS  ACT_SEATS
------ ------------ -------------- ---------- ---------
     1 Boeing 747   Wide           Double           416
```

Just as with the English language, double-negatives are possible. They should be avoided because they make the intent of the SQL harder to determine. The following statement returns rows where the number of decks is NOT not-equal to 'Single'. A query where the decks were equal to 'Single' would be much easier to read.

```
SELECT *
FROM   aircraft_types
WHERE  NOT act_decks != 'Single';

ACT_ID ACT_NAME     ACT_BODY_STYLE ACT_DECKS  ACT_SEATS
------ ------------ -------------- ---------- ---------
     2 Boeing 767   Wide           Single           350
     3 Boeing 737   Narrow         Single           200
     4 Boeing 757   Narrow         Single           240
```

**Precedence in WHERE clauses**

When evaluating a WHERE clause, the order in which Oracle executes each of the conditions and operations is of critical importance in what the final result will be. The rules of precedence according to the Oracle SQL Reference manual are:

1. Arithmetic Operators (+, - , *, /)
2. Concatenation Operator (||)
3. Comparison conditions (=, !=, <, >, <=, >=)
4. IS [NOT] NULL, LIKE, [NOT] BETWEEN, [NOT] IN, EXISTS, IS OF type
5. NOT logical condition
6. AND logical condition
7. OR logical condition

You can override the default order of precedence by making use of parenthesis. When you have a particularly complex clause, adding parenthesis is often advisable even if not strictly required in order to make the order of precedence more evident.

## Use ampersand substitution to restrict and sort output at runtime

The ampersand symbol '&' is used in the SQL*Plus and SQL Developer tools to add a substitution variable to a SQL statement. Substitution variables allow you to build scripts that are not 100% fixed to run the same way every time they are executed. By replacing portions of one or more parts of a SQL statement with ampersands, you can cause the tool to replace those elements of the SQL with data that will be supplied at run-time. Substitution variables can be used to replace the following:

- Column Expressions
- Table names
- WHERE conditions

- ORDER BY clauses
- Complete SELECT statements

When the following SQL statement is executed, a dialog box will open up requesting a value for the substitution variable AIRCRAFT_NAME. Note that the substitution variable is enclosed in quotes. The tool will take the information you supply, swap it for the substitution variable verbatim, and then run the SQL. Since the below statement is a character field, it must be enclosed in quotes. If the substitution variable were not enclosed in quotes, you would have to quote the value entered in the dialog or the statement would result in an error.

```
SELECT act_name, act_body_style, act_decks
FROM   aircraft_types
WHERE  act_name = '&AIRCRAFT_NAME';
```

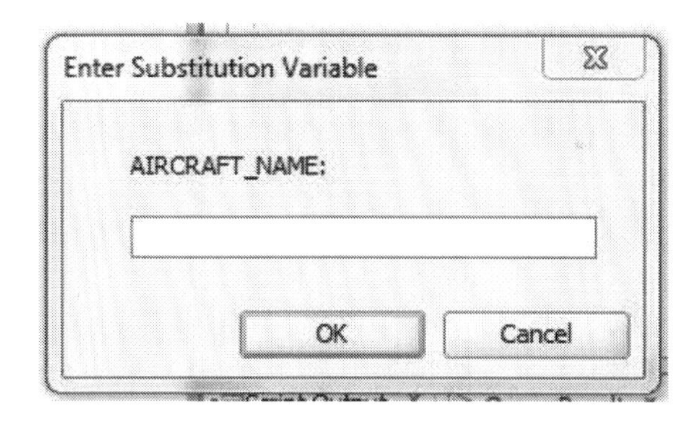


Once the dialog box has been populated and the OK button clicked, the query will continue and produce results with the new value. By default, the tool will also provide information about the replacement that was just performed. From this, you can see that '&AIRCRAFT_NAME' became 'Boeing'. Nothing else in the SQL statement (including the enclosing quotes) was altered

```
old:SELECT act_name, act_body_style, act_decks
FROM   aircraft_types
WHERE  act_name = '&AIRCRAFT_NAME'
new:SELECT act_name, act_body_style, act_decks
FROM   aircraft_types
WHERE  act_name = 'Boeing 767';

ACT_NAME     ACT_BODY_STYLE ACT_DECKS
------------ -------------- ----------
Boeing 767   Wide           Single
```

The following example has substitution variables set up for a column, a WHERE clause condition, and the ORDER BY clause. The user can specify each of these values at run time:

```
SELECT apt_name, apt_abbr, act_name, &COLUMN_NAME
FROM   aircraft_fleet_v
WHERE  &WHERE_CLAUSE
ORDER BY &ORDER_BY;
```

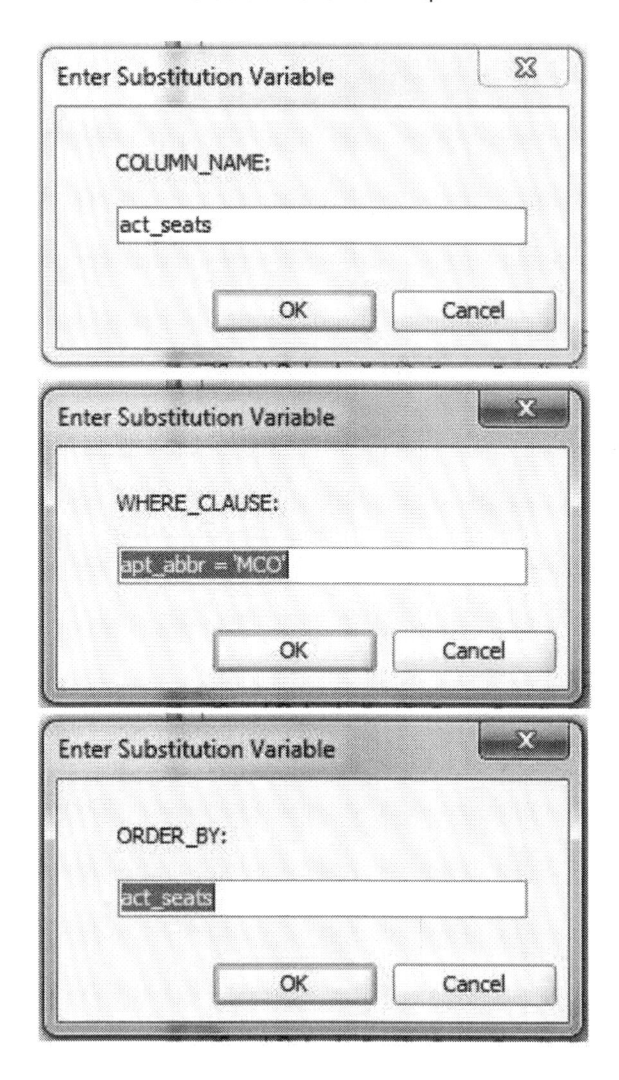


```
old:SELECT apt_name, apt_abbr, act_name, &COLUMN_NAME
FROM   aircraft_fleet_v
WHERE  &WHERE_CLAUSE
ORDER BY &ORDER_BY
new:SELECT apt_name, apt_abbr, act_name, act_seats
FROM   aircraft_fleet_v
WHERE  apt_abbr = 'MCO'
ORDER BY act_seats

APT_NAME               APT_ABBR ACT_NAME     ACT_SEATS
---------------------- -------- ------------ ---------
Orlando, FL            MCO      Boeing 767         350
Orlando, FL            MCO      Boeing 767         350
```

The text returned by SQL*Plus and SQL Developer that shows the old and new versions of a SQL statement using substitution variables is part of the VERIFY function. You can disable this capability by issuing the command SET VERIFY OFF. Likewise, if you have disabled it but wish to re-enable it, you can issue the SET VERIFY ON command.

All of the examples so far have used one variant of the substitution variable. Substitution variables can be specified with either a single ampersand or with a pair of ampersands. The behavior difference is that when a substitution variable is specified with two ampersands, it is possible to re-use the variable in another portion of the statement without having to prompt the user again. The value is persistent, in fact, not just for the remainder of the statement but for the Oracle session as well. If the script were to be run a second time, the user would not be prompted for the variable. Only the first occurrence of the column needs to have the double-ampersand. Once it has been set, it can be referenced again using either a single or double ampersand.

```
SELECT apt_name, apt_abbr, act_name, &&COLUMN_NAME
FROM   aircraft_fleet_v
ORDER BY &COLUMN_NAME;
```

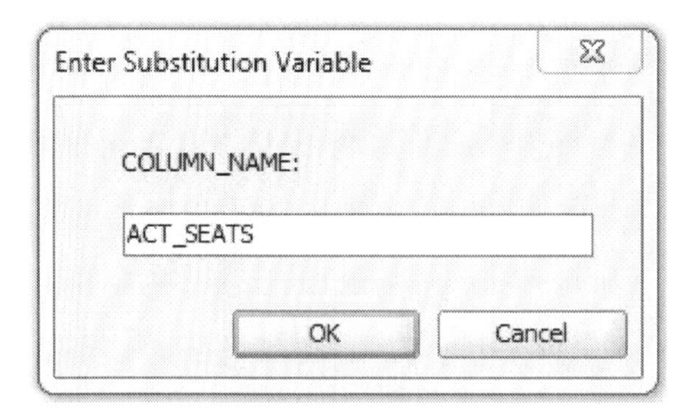

```
APT_NAME               APT_ABBR ACT_NAME     ACT_SEATS
---------------------- -------- ------------ ---------
Atlanta, GA            ATL      Boeing 737         200
Atlanta, GA            ATL      Boeing 757         240
Orlando, FL            MCO      Boeing 767         350
Dallas/Fort Worth      DFW      Boeing 767         350
Orlando, FL            MCO      Boeing 767         350
Dallas/Fort Worth      DFW      Boeing 747         416
Miami, FL              MIA      Boeing 747         416
Miami, FL              MIA      Boeing 747         416
```

**DEFINE and UNDEFINE**

The DEFINE command is used to set a substitution variable to a given value. If the DEFINE command is used to set the value of a variable prior to running a SQL statement that makes use of it, the user won't be prompted for the value. The double-ampersand works by accepting the variable supplied by the user, and then performing an implicit DEFINE so that the value won't be requested again in the current session. The UNDEFINE command is used to clear a substitution variable value (so that the next SQL statement using that variable will prompt the user for a value).

```
DEFINE variable_name
UNDEFINE variable_name
```

## Use SQL row limiting clause

Two new clauses were added to the SELECT command in the Oracle 12c release: FETCH FIRST and OFFSET. The FETCH FIRST clause limits the number of rows returned by a given query. The OFFSET clause allows you to specify a starting row for the return set. FETCH FIRST and OFFSET simplify syntax and comply with the ANSI SQL standard.

A common database reporting requirement is the need to generate a 'Top-N' result set. Examples include the top five highest-paid employees, the top ten selling products and so forth. While there have been several ways to generate this data in earlier releases, until 12c, there has been no native SQL syntax designed for this. Commonly people have attempted to use the ROWNUM pseudocolumn to generate a 'Top-N' result set. This does not generate the correct results because the WHERE clause is evaluated before the ORDER BY clause. Essentially the below query takes the first five unsorted rows returned by the query and <u>then</u> orders them. It is <u>possible</u> to force Oracle to sort the rows first, but not straightforward.

```
SELECT apt_name, apt_abbr, act_name
FROM   aircraft_fleet_v
WHERE  rownum < 6
ORDER BY apt_name, act_name

APT_NAME               APT_ABBR ACT_NAME
---------------------- -------- --------------------
Dallas/Fort Worth      DFW      Boeing 747
Dallas/Fort Worth      DFW      Boeing 767
Miami, FL              MIA      Boeing 747
Miami, FL              MIA      Boeing 747
Orlando, FL            MCO      Boeing 767
```

The FETCH FIRST and OFFSET operations take place after the ORDER BY clause has been executed. This makes generating this type of information simpler and more intuitive. The following example uses the FETCH FIRST clause to return only the first five aircraft ordered by airport name and then aircraft name in the AIRPORT_FLEET_V view.

```
SELECT apt_name, apt_abbr, act_name
FROM   aircraft_fleet_v
ORDER BY apt_name, act_name
FETCH FIRST 5 ROWS ONLY;

APT_NAME               APT_ABBR ACT_NAME
---------------------- -------- -----------
Atlanta, GA            ATL      Boeing 737
Atlanta, GA            ATL      Boeing 757
Dallas/Fort Worth      DFW      Boeing 747
Dallas/Fort Worth      DFW      Boeing 767
Miami, FL              MIA      Boeing 747
```

The OFFSET syntax expands this functionality to allow you to pull a set of rows in the middle of the available data (for example the 20th through the 25th highest paid employees). The following example uses the same data and order as the above query, but skips the first three rows and then pulls the next four (i.e. the fourth through the seventh row). Note that the first two rows in this query match the last two in the query above.

```
SELECT apt_name, apt_abbr, act_name
FROM   aircraft_fleet_v
ORDER BY apt_name, act_name
OFFSET 3 FETCH NEXT 4 ROWS NLY;

Dallas/Fort Worth       DFW      Boeing 767
Miami, FL               MIA      Boeing 747
Miami, FL               MIA      Boeing 747
Orlando, FL             MCO      Boeing 767
```

The FETCH FIRST syntax does not itself look for high or low values but rather returns the rows as they are retrieved based on the sort order. Sorting the same data in the reverse order produces the five aircraft that sorted to the bottom of the initial query. The FETCH FIRST syntax does exactly what it indicates, return the first 'x' number of rows from a query – whatever those rows contain.

```
SELECT apt_name, apt_abbr, act_name
FROM   aircraft_fleet_v
ORDER BY apt_name DESC, act_name DESC
FETCH FIRST 5 ROWS ONLY;

APT_NAME                APT_ABBR ACT_NAME
----------------------- -------- ----------
Orlando, FL             MCO      Boeing 767
Orlando, FL             MCO      Boeing 767
Miami, FL               MIA      Boeing 747
Miami, FL               MIA      Boeing 747
Dallas/Fort Worth       DFW      Boeing 767
```

When used by itself, the ONLY keyword will return the exact number of rows specified in the FECTH FIRST clause (unless the table contains fewer rows than the number specified of course). However, when used in conjunction with the 'WITH TIES' syntax, a FETCH FIRST query can return more than the specified number if the query result set contains rows with values in the ORDER BY column(s) that are equal. For example, the following query is similar to the initial query, but contains the WITH TIES syntax. Because the fifth and sixth rows have the same airport and aircraft names, the query returns six rows rather than five.

```
SELECT apt_name, apt_abbr, act_name
FROM   aircraft_fleet_v
ORDER BY apt_name, act_name
FETCH FIRST 5 ROWS ONLY WITH TIES;

APT_NAME               APT_ABBR ACT_NAME
---------------------- -------- ----------
Atlanta, GA            ATL      Boeing 737
Atlanta, GA            ATL      Boeing 757
Dallas/Fort Worth      DFW      Boeing 747
Dallas/Fort Worth      DFW      Boeing 767
Miami, FL              MIA      Boeing 747
Miami, FL              MIA      Boeing 747
```

It is also possible to supply a percentage of rows to be fetched instead of a value. However, a percentage value cannot be used for the offset. The following example returns the first twenty-five percent of rows returned by the query. The AIRCRAFT_FLEET_V view contains eight rows total, so two rows are returned.

```
SELECT apt_name, apt_abbr, act_name
FROM   aircraft_fleet_v
ORDER BY apt_name, act_name
FETCH FIRST 25 PERCENT ROWS ONLY;

APT_NAME               APT_ABBR ACT_NAME
---------------------- -------- ----------
Atlanta, GA            ATL      Boeing 737
Atlanta, GA            ATL      Boeing 757
```

# Using Single-Row Functions to Customize Output

## Use various types of functions available in SQL

Functions are an extremely important part of Oracle's capabilities. Functions will sometimes accept one or more arguments, but they will always return a value when called. When a single row function is included in a SQL query, it will generate one result for each table row returned. By contrast, a multiple-row function will return one result for a given set of rows. Single row functions can be used in the following locations:

- SELECT lists
- WHERE clauses
- START WITH clauses
- CONNECT BY clauses
- HAVING clauses
- ORDER BY clauses

SQL functions are built into the Oracle Database and can be used in various SQL statements. SQL functions should not be confused with user-defined functions written in PL/SQL. There are too many SQL functions available in Oracle to discuss all of them in this guide. I'll define some of the more common ones that might appear on the test. Before attempting the test, you should investigate the SQL Functions in the Oracle SQL Language Reference book. You are almost certain to see some on the test that are not in this guide and you will need some familiarity with what they do.

There are five distinct types of single row functions available in Oracle.

- **Numeric** – Accept numeric input and return numeric results.
- **Character** – Accept character input and return character or numeric results.
- **Datetime** – Perform work on date data types and return date or numeric results.
- **Conversion** – Convert from one data type to another.

- **General** – Perform operations that don't fit any of the above four descriptions.

## Numeric Functions

### ABS

**Syntax:** ABS(*n*)

**Purpose:** ABS returns the absolute value of *n*.

```
SELECT ABS(-5) "Abs_Ex"
FROM   dual;

Abs_Ex
----------
5
```

### CEIL

**Syntax:** CEIL(*n*)

**Purpose:** CEIL returns the smallest integer that is greater than or equal to *n*.

```
SELECT CEIL(2343.2) "Ceil_Ex"
FROM   dual;

Ceil_Ex
-----------
2344
```

### FLOOR

**Syntax:** FLOOR(*n*)

**Purpose:** FLOOR returns the largest integer equal to or less than *n*.

```
SELECT FLOOR(21.2) "Floor_Ex"
FROM   dual;

Floor_Ex
----------
21
```

## ROUND(number)

**Syntax:** ROUND(*n, integer*)

**Purpose:** ROUND returns *n* rounded to *integer* places to the right of the decimal point. If *integer* is not supplied, then *n* is rounded to zero places. If the *integer* value is negative, then *n* is rounded off to the left of the decimal point.

```
SELECT ROUND(127.623, 1)  "Round_Ex1",
       ROUND(127.623)     "Round_Ex2",
       ROUND(127.623, -1) "Round_Ex3"
FROM   dual;

Round_Ex1  Round_Ex2  Round_Ex3
---------- ---------- ----------
     127.6        128        130
```

## SIGN(number)

**Syntax:** SIGN(*n*)

**Purpose:** SIGN returns the sign of n. This function takes as an argument any numeric data type, or any nonnumeric data type that can be implicitly converted to NUMBER, and returns NUMBER.

For a supplied value of type NUMBER, the result is:

- -1 if n<0
- 0 if n=0
- 1 if n>0

For binary floating-point numbers (BINARY_FLOAT and BINARY_DOUBLE), the function will return the sign bit of the number. The sign bit is:

- -1 if n<0
- +1 if n>=0 or n=NaN

### Character Functions

Character functions can return either a character value or a numeric value. Some of those which return a character value are:

### INITCAP

**Syntax:** INITCAP(*char*)

**Purpose:** INITCAP returns *char*, with the first letter of each word in uppercase, and all other letters in lowercase. The delimiter used to determine words are white space or non alphanumeric characters.

```
SELECT INITCAP('john jones') "Initcap_Ex"
FROM   dual;

Initcap_Ex
---------
John Jones
```

### LOWER

**Syntax:** LOWER ( *char* )

**Purpose:** LOWER returns *char*, with all letters lowercase.

```
SELECT LOWER('John Jones') "Lower_Ex"
FROM   dual;

Lower_EX
----------------
john jones
```

### LPAD

**Syntax:** LPAD(*expr1, n, expr2*)

**Purpose:** LPAD returns *expr1*, left-padded to length *n* characters with the sequence of characters in *expr2*. If *expr2* is not specified, then the default value is a single space.

```
SELECT LPAD('Page 1', 14, '.') "Lpad_Ex"
FROM   dual;

Lpad_Ex
---------------
........Page 1
```

### LTRIM

**Syntax:** LTRIM(*char, set*)

**Purpose:** LTRIM removes from the left end of *char* all of the characters contained in *set*. If *set* is not specified, it defaults to a single space.

```
SELECT LTRIM('\----/DATA\----/', '/\-') "Ltrim_Ex"
FROM   dual;

Ltrim_Ex
----------
DATA\----/
```

### SUBSTR

**Syntax:** SUBSTR(*char, position, substring_length*)

**Purpose:** The SUBSTR functions return a portion of char, beginning at character position, substring_length characters long. SUBSTR calculates lengths using characters as defined by the input character set.

```
SELECT SUBSTR('Jack and Jill went up the hill', 10, 4) "Substr_Ex"
FROM   dual;

Substr_Ex
---------
Jill
```

The following character functions return a numeric value.

### ASCII

**Syntax:** ASCII(*char*)

**Purpose:** ASCII returns the decimal representation in the database character set of the first character of char.

```
SELECT ASCII('G') "Ascii_Ex"
FROM   dual;

Ascii_Ex
--------
      71
```

### LENGTH

**Syntax:** LENGTH(*char*)

**Purpose:** The LENGTH functions return the length of *char*. LENGTH calculates length using characters as defined by the input character set.

```
SELECT LENGTH('1Z0-047') "Length_Ex"
FROM   dual;

Length_Ex
----------
7
```

## Datetime Functions

### ADD_MONTHS

**Syntax:** ADD_MONTHS(*date, integer*)

**Purpose:** ADD_MONTHS returns the supplied *date* plus *integer* months.

```
SELECT TO_CHAR(ADD_MONTHS('10-MAR-11', 1), 'DD-MON-YY')
"Add_months_Ex"
FROM   dual;

Add_months_Ex
-------------
10-APR-11
```

### LAST_DAY

**Syntax:** LAST_DAY(*date*)

**Purpose:** Returns the last day of the month that contains *date*.

```
SELECT LAST_DAY('12-MAR-11') "Last_day_Ex"
FROM   dual;

Last_day_Ex
-----------
31-MAR-11
```

### MONTHS_BETWEEN

**Syntax:** MONTHS_BETWEEN(*date1, date2*)

**Purpose:** MONTHS_BETWEEN returns number of months between *date1* and *date2*. If *date1* is later than *date2*, then the result is positive. If *date1* is earlier than *date2*, then the result is negative. If *date1* and *date2* are either the same days of the month or both last days of months, then the result is an integer.

```
SELECT MONTHS_BETWEEN('02-JAN-12', '04-JUN-12') "Months_Between_Ex"
FROM   dual;

Months_Between_Ex
------------------
-5.06451612903225806451612903225806451613
```

## NEXT_DAY

**Syntax:** NEXT_DAY(*date*, *char*)

**Purpose:** NEXT_DAY returns the date of the first weekday named by *char* that is later than *date*. The return type is always DATE, regardless of the data type of date.

```
SELECT NEXT_DAY('03-MAR-12','FRIDAY') "Next_day_Ex"
FROM   dual;

Next_day_Ex
--------------
09-MAR-12
```

## Conversion Functions

## TO_NUMBER

**Syntax:** TO_NUMBER(expr, fmt, 'nlsparam')

**Purpose:** TO_NUMBER converts expr to a value of NUMBER data type. The expr can be a BINARY_DOUBLE value or a value of character data type containing a number in the format specified by the optional format model fmt. The optional 'nlsparam' argument specifies the language in which the number format is returned.

```
SELECT TO_NUMBER('$4,355.80', 'FML999G990D00') "To_Num_Ex"
FROM   dual;

To_Num_Ex
---------
4355.8
```

## TO_CHAR

**Syntax:** TO_CHAR(datetime, fmt, 'nlsparam')

**Purpose:** Converts a datetime to a value of VARCHAR2 data type in the format specified by the date format fmt. The optional 'nlsparam' argument specifies the language in which month and day names and abbreviations are returned.

```
SELECT TO_CHAR(SYSDATE, 'Day, Month DD, YYYY') AS "To_Char_Ex"
FROM   dual;

To_Char_Ex
------------------------------
Saturday , April     07, 2012
```

## TO_DATE

**Syntax:** TO_DATE(char, fmt, 'nlsparam')

**Purpose**: TO_DATE converts char of a character data type to a value of DATE data type. The fmt is a datetime model format specifying the format of char. The 'nlsparam' argument specifies the language of the text string that is being converted to a date.

```
SELECT TO_DATE('Saturday , April     07, 2012 ',
               'Day, Month DD, YYYY') AS "To_Date_Ex"
FROM   dual;

To_Date_Ex
----------
07-APR-12
```

## General Functions

### NVL

**Syntax:** NVL(expr1, expr2)

**Purpose:** NVL will replace NULL with a string. If expr1 is NULL, then NVL returns expr2. If expr1 is not NULL, then NVL returns expr1.

```
SELECT NVL('', 'Value is NULL') "Nvl_Ex1",
       NVL(dummy, 'Value is NULL') "Nvl_Ex2"
FROM   dual;

Nvl_Ex1       Nvl_Ex2
------------- -------------
Value is NULL X
```

### NULLIF

**Syntax:** NULLIF(expr1, expr2)

**Purpose:** If expr1 and expr2 are equal, then NULLIF returns null. If they are not equal, then is returns expr1. You cannot specify the literal NULL for expr1.

```
SELECT NULLIF(dummy, 'X') "Nullif_Ex2"
FROM   dual;

Nullif_Ex2
----------
```

## Use character, number, date and analytical functions in SELECT statements

### Character Functions

The character functions of Oracle modify or provide information regarding character data types in Oracle. Character SQL functions can be used in the SELECT clause in order to modify the data returned by a statement. The following function transforms airport names to upper-case:

```
SELECT UPPER(apt_name) APT_NAME, apt_abbr
FROM   airports;

APT_NAME                       APT_ABBR
------------------------------ --------
ORLANDO, FL                    MCO
ATLANTA, GA                    ATL
MIAMI, FL                      MIA
JACKSONVILLE, FL               JAX
DALLAS/FORT WORTH              DFW
```

The INITCAP function works similarly to the UPPER function except that it capitalizes only the initial letter of each word:

```
SELECT INITCAP(apt_name) APT_NAME, apt_abbr
FROM   airports;

APT_NAME               APT_ABBR
---------------------- --------
Orlando, Fl            MCO
Atlanta, Ga            ATL
Miami, Fl              MIA
Jacksonville, Fl       JAX
Dallas/Fort Worth      DFW
```

People often use INITCAP as a means of capitalizing names. It works reasonably well for that in most cases. However, in others, it does not properly handle the name. When you make use of functions, you need to understand their behavior and consider how it will apply to your data.

```
SELECT INITCAP('THURSTON HOWELL, III') "Initcap_Fail_Ex"
FROM   dual;

Initcap_Fail_Ex
--------------------
Thurston Howell, Iii
```

You can also use SQL functions in the WHERE clause to create custom conditions that will locate specific rows. In the example below, the airport name is upper cased, and then the third character pulled out via the SUBSTR function to return all airports with an 'L' as the third letter. This is a common method for making a case-insensitive query.

```
SELECT apt_name, apt_abbr
FROM   airports
WHERE  SUBSTR(UPPER(apt_name), 3, 1) = 'L';

APT_NAME                       APT_ABBR
------------------------------ --------
Orlando, FL                    MCO
Atlanta, GA                    ATL
Dallas/Fort Worth              DFW
```

**Numeric Functions**

Just as character functions alter or provide information about character data, numeric functions perform operations against numeric data. Unlike character and date functions, numeric functions always accept a numeric value and always return a numeric value. In the following example, the annual salary of employees is divided by the number of hours in a work year, and the result rounded to two decimal places with the ROUND function:

```
SELECT emp_first, emp_last, ROUND(salary / 2080, 2) AS HOURLY_SAL
FROM   employees
WHERE  emp_job = 'Pilot';
```

```
EMP_FIRST  EMP_LAST   HOURLY_SAL
---------- ---------- ----------
John       Jones           46.88
Top        Gun             43.99
Phil       McCoy           50.48
James      Thomas          47.36
John       Picard           23.8
Luke       Skytalker       43.27
Dell       Aptop           42.07
Noh        Kia             44.35
```

The TRUNC function performs a function similar ROUND. However, where the ROUND function will perform a rounding operation on decimal values to the right of the defined precision, TRUNC simply removes all numbers to the right of the defined precision. In the example below, Jones, Thomas, Picard, Skytalker, and Aptop are all shown a penny lower because the tenths of a penny were truncated rather than being rounded.

```
SELECT emp_first, emp_last, TRUNC(salary / 2080, 2) AS HOURLY_SAL
FROM   employees
WHERE  emp_job = 'Pilot';

EMP_FIRST  EMP_LAST   HOURLY_SAL
---------- ---------- ----------
John       Jones           46.87
Top        Gun             43.99
Phil       McCoy           50.48
James      Thomas          47.35
John       Picard          23.79
Luke       Skytalker       43.26
Dell       Aptop           42.06
Noh        Kia             44.35
```

**Date Functions**

As mentioned earlier, Oracle stores date data in an internal format that contains century, year, month, day, hours, minutes, and seconds. The Oracle date model can store dates between January 1, 4712 B.C. and December 31, 9999 A.D. That means that in a little less than 8000 years, someone is going to predict the world will end on Dec 31, 9999 because Larry Ellison said it would.

Date SQL functions are used to transform information in DATE data types. In the below example, the MONTHS_BETWEEN function is used to determine the number of months it has been since each of the pilots was hired. Note that while two DATE types are passed to the function, a NUMBER type is returned. The value returned by SQL DATE functions is not always the same as the value passed to it.

```
SELECT emp_first, emp_last,
       MONTHS_BETWEEN(SYSDATE, start_date) AS months_since_hire
FROM   employees
WHERE  emp_job = 'Pilot';

EMP_FIRST      EMP_LAST        MONTHS_SINCE_HIRE
-------------- --------------- ------------------
John           Jones           203.57773484169653524492234169
Top            Gun             185.48096064814814814814814814
Phil           McCoy           189.60999290621266427718040621
James          Thomas          154.51321871266427718040621266
John           Picard          124.54547677718040621266427718
Luke           Skytalker       114.57773484169653524492234169
Dell           Aptop           103.19063806750298685782556750
Noh            Kia             92.674509035244922341696535244
```

The MONTH_SINCE_HIRE value is really awkward in the above example. Because the result of the MONTHS_BETWEEN function is a NUMBER type, we can apply the numeric function TRUNC to the result to clean it up:

```
SELECT emp_first, emp_last,
       TRUNC(MONTHS_BETWEEN(SYSDATE, start_date)) AS
months_since_hire
FROM   employees
WHERE  emp_job = 'Pilot';

EMP_FIRST      EMP_LAST        MONTHS_SINCE_HIRE
-------------- ---------------- ------------------
John           Jones                          203
Top            Gun                            185
Phil           McCoy                          189
James          Thomas                         154
John           Picard                         124
Luke           Skytalker                      114
Dell           Aptop                          103
Noh            Kia                             92
```

## Performing Date Calculations

Not only is the Oracle date format numeric, but it is stored in such a way that a single day equals one. The means that if you take a given date value and add the number three to it, the resulting value is exactly three days later than the original date value. Likewise you can subtract three from a given date and the result date will be exactly three days prior to the original. The following two examples demonstrate adding and subtracting the number three from the current date.

```
SELECT TO_CHAR(SYSDATE, 'DD-MON HH24:MI:SS') AS SYS_DATE,
       TO_CHAR(SYSDATE + 3, 'DD-MON HH24:MI:SS') AS SYS_DATE_P3
FROM   dual;

SYS_DATE                  SYS_DATE_P3
------------------------- ------------------------
07-APR 21:28:10           10-APR 21:28:10
```

```
SELECT TO_CHAR(SYSDATE, 'DD-MON HH24:MI:SS') AS SYS_DATE,
       TO_CHAR(SYSDATE - 3, 'DD-MON HH24:MI:SS') AS SYS_DATE_M3
FROM   dual;

SYS_DATE                  SYS_DATE_M3
------------------------- ------------------------
07-APR 21:28:42           04-APR 21:28:42
```

Just as the number one represents a single day, fractions of 1 represent a fraction of a day. To add or subtract hours from a date, you can use increments of 1/24 (one hour). To add or subtract minutes from a date, you can use increments of 1/1440 (there are 1440 minutes in a day). The following two examples demonstrate this. The first subtracts seven hours from the current date, and the second subtracts 22 minutes.

```
SELECT TO_CHAR(SYSDATE, 'DD-MON HH24:MI:SS') AS SYS_DATE,
       TO_CHAR(SYSDATE - 7/24, 'DD-MON HH24:MI:SS')
              AS SYS_DATE_TR
FROM   dual;
```

```
SYS_DATE                  SYS_DATE_TR
------------------------- ------------------------
07-APR 21:29:16           07-APR 14:29:16


SELECT TO_CHAR(SYSDATE, 'DD-MON HH24:MI:SS') AS SYS_DATE,
       TO_CHAR(SYSDATE - 22/1440, 'DD-MON HH24:MI:SS')
              AS SYS_DATE_TR
FROM   dual;

SYS_DATE                  SYS_DATE_TR
------------------------- ------------------------
07-APR 21:33:52           07-APR 21:11:52
```

One interesting function not normally associated with dates is TRUNC. Because dates are numeric, the TRUNC function can be used to modify the date value. When applied against a date with no format specified, it removes the decimal portion (the part of a day past midnight). When a format is supplied, you can truncate to the start of the most recent hour, month or year (among other possibilities). It's also possible to use the ROUND function with dates.

```
SELECT TO_CHAR(SYSDATE, 'DD-MON HH24:MI:SS') AS SYS_DATE,
       TO_CHAR(TRUNC(SYSDATE), 'DD-MON HH24:MI:SS')
              AS TRUNC_DAY
FROM   dual;

SYS_DATE                  TRUNC_DAY
------------------------- ------------------------
07-APR 21:42:54           07-APR 00:00:00


SELECT TO_CHAR(SYSDATE, 'DD-MON HH24:MI:SS') AS SYS_DATE,
       TO_CHAR(TRUNC(SYSDATE, 'HH'), 'DD-MON HH24:MI:SS')
              AS TRUNC_HOUR
FROM   dual;

SYS_DATE                  TRUNC_HOUR
------------------------- ------------------------
07-APR 21:42:54           07-APR 21:00:00


SELECT TO_CHAR(SYSDATE, 'DD-MON HH24:MI:SS') AS SYS_DATE,
       TO_CHAR(TRUNC(SYSDATE, 'MM'), 'DD-MON HH24:MI:SS')
              AS TRUNC_MONTH
FROM   dual;
```

```
SYS_DATE                 TRUNC_MONTH
------------------------ ------------------------
07-APR 21:43:26          01-APR 00:00:00


SELECT TO_CHAR(SYSDATE, 'DD-MON HH24:MI:SS') AS SYS_DATE,
       TO_CHAR(TRUNC(SYSDATE, 'YYYY'), 'DD-MON HH24:MI:SS')
              AS TRUNC_YEAR
FROM   dual;

SYS_DATE                 TRUNC_YEAR
------------------------ ------------------------
07-APR 21:43:49          01-JAN 00:00:00
```

**RR date Format**

This date format was a product of the Y2K hysteria in the late 90s. For years two digits had been used as shorthand to represent a four-digit year (01-JAN-71 instead of 01-JAN-1971). Suddenly, everyone realized that the millennium was about to end and reset the numbering scheme. Programs that simply added the current millennium and century to a two-digit year would produce a date that was 100 years off from what was originally intended.

The RR date format was designed to allow existing interfaces with two-digit years to be used and have the database logically determine what millennium and century the user intended. The RR logic makes use of the current two-digit year and compares it to the supplied two-digit year to determine what was meant.

- If current year is 0-49 (i.e. 2000-2049) and supplied year is 0-49, use current century.
- If current year is 50-99 (i.e. 2050-2099) and supplied year is 50-99, use current century.
- If current year is 0-49 and supplied year is 50-99, use prior century.
- If current year is 50-99 and supplied year is 0-49, use next century.

Keep in mind that this logic isn't always correct. For example, it would make the wrong choice if you were entering a birth date into Oracle for someone who was born in 1932. The RR logic would store this value as 2032. For numbers that can span decades, you should really make use of a four-digit year so that there is no ambiguity whatsoever in the meaning.

## Analytic Functions

The Oracle test development team arguably could have put analytic functions either in this section with single-row functions or in the next section on using the group functions to report on aggregated data. Analytic functions are somewhere in-between the two. Single-row functions produce one value per row processed and act only on data in that row. Aggregate functions act on groups of rows and return one result per group. The following two queries against the AIRCRAFT_TYPES table make use of a single-row function and aggregate function respectively:

```
SELECT UPPER(act_body_style) ACT_BODY_STYLE, act_seats
FROM   aircraft_types;

ACT_BODY_STYLE  ACT_SEATS
-------------- ----------
WIDE                  416
WIDE                  350
NARROW                200
NARROW                240
WIDE                  407
WIDE                  296
NARROW                200
WIDE                  525

SELECT act_body_style, AVG(act_seats) AVG_SEATS
FROM   aircraft_types
GROUP BY act_body_style;

ACT_BODY_STYLE  AVG_SEATS
-------------- ----------
Wide                398.8
Narrow         213.333333
```

Analytic functions act like aggregate functions in that they generate a value based on a group of rows rather than a single row. However, instead of returning a single row for each grouping, analytic functions return one result per row acted on by the query. The following example executes an aggregate function against the AIRCRAFT_TYPES table. The result of the function is similar to the aggregate example above, but the number of rows is the same as was returned by the single-row function above:

```
SELECT act_body_style, act_seats,
       AVG(act_seats) OVER (PARTITION BY act_body_style) AVG_BY_STYLE
FROM   aircraft_types;

ACT_BODY_STYLE  ACT_SEATS AVG_BY_STYLE
-------------- ---------- ------------
Narrow                240   213.333333
Narrow                200   213.333333
Narrow                200   213.333333
Wide                  525        398.8
Wide                  407        398.8
Wide                  296        398.8
Wide                  350        398.8
Wide                  416        398.8
```

The grouped rows in an analytic query are called a window. The window of rows is not set but rather slides based on the row currently being acted on by the function. For example, the analytic function might include ten rows above and ten rows below the current row when calculating a value. The size of the window can be either a count of rows or a logical interval such as time. The SQL engine processes analytic functions immediately prior to the ORDER BY clause (and after the WHERE, GROUP BY, and HAVING clauses). For this reason, they can only appear in the SELECT list of a query.

The basic syntax for an analytic function is as follows.

```
analytic_function([ arguments ]) OVER (analytic_clause)
```

The analytic_clause can contain the following optional elements.

```
[ query_partition_clause ] [ order_by_clause [ windowing_clause ] ]
```

The query_partition_clause serves to partition the query result set into groups based on one or more expressions. When omitted, the function will treat all rows returned by the query as a single group. It is possible to have multiple analytic functions in the same query, and the PARTITION BY keys can be the same or different for each. The expressions used in the query_partition_clause can be constants, columns, nonanalytic functions, function expressions, or expressions involving any of these. The following example uses the same query from above with a blank query_partition_clause to generate the average number of seats across all aircraft:

```
SELECT act_body_style, act_seats,
       AVG(act_seats) OVER () AVG_OVER_ALL
FROM   aircraft_types;

ACT_BODY_STYLE  ACT_SEATS AVG_OVER_ALL
-------------- ---------- ------------
Wide                  416       329.25
Wide                  350       329.25
Narrow                200       329.25
Narrow                240       329.25
Wide                  407       329.25
Wide                  296       329.25
Narrow                200       329.25
Wide                  525       329.25
```

The order_by_clause is utilized to order the rows within a partition. It is possible to order the values in the partitions for all analytic functions on one or more keys. Each key is defined by an expression and can be qualified by an ordering sequence. The following example shows the result of ordering the AIRCRAFT_TYPES query by the ACT_SEAT column:

```
SELECT act_body_style, act_seats,
       AVG(act_seats) OVER (PARTITION BY act_body_style ORDER BY
act_seats) AVG_BY_STYLE
FROM   aircraft_types;
```

```
ACT_BODY_STYLE  ACT_SEATS AVG_BY_STYLE
-------------- ---------- ------------
Narrow                200          200
Narrow                200          200
Narrow                240   213.333333
Wide                  296          296
Wide                  350          323
Wide                  407          351
Wide                  416       367.25
Wide                  525        398.8
```

Many but not all of the analytic functions allow the windowing_clause. This clause allows more control over the window used in calculating the function value. Some of the options allowed in this clause include:

- **ROWS | RANGE** -- Define the a window used for calculating the function result for each row. ROWS specifies the window in physical units (rows). RANGE specifies the window as a logical offset. In order to use this clause, the function must also specify an order_by_clause.
- **BETWEEN ... AND** -- This clause is used to specify a start point and end point for the window.
- **UNBOUNDED PRECEDING** -- This indicates that the window starts at the first row of the partition.
- **UNBOUNDED FOLLOWING** -- This indicates that the window ends at the last row of the partition.
- **CURRENT ROW** -- This can be used to specify that the window begins at the current row or value (depending on whether you have specified ROW or RANGE) or the end row or value of the range.

There are around fifty analytic functions defined in the Oracle 12c SQL Reference manual. You should reference the documentation for more examples. Following are more details on the handful specifically noted in the section title:

## PERCENTILE_CONT

This function accepts a percentile value and a sort specification, and returns an interpolated value that would fall into that percentile value with respect to the sort specification. Any NULL values in the data are ignored. The 'CONT' suffix means that the function assumes a continuous distribution model. There is a PERCENTILE_DISC function that assumes a discrete distribution model. The difference between the two models gets deeper into statistics than the exam (or this guide) will get into. Google it if you are particularly interested.

The following example uses the PERCENTILE_CONT function to calculate the value that is at the midpoint of the window for Narrow and Wide body styles. For Narrow, the middle row has a value of 200 seats and for Wide it it 407.

```
SELECT act_body_style, act_seats,
       PERCENTILE_CONT(0.5) WITHIN GROUP (ORDER BY act_seats)
       OVER (PARTITION BY act_body_style) PC_BY_STYLE
FROM   aircraft_types;

ACT_BODY_STYLE  ACT_SEATS PC_BY_STYLE
-------------- ---------- -----------
Narrow                200         200
Narrow                200         200
Narrow                240         200
Wide                  296         407
Wide                  350         407
Wide                  407         407
Wide                  416         407
Wide                  525         407
```

## STDDEV

This function generates the sample standard deviation of a supplied expression. The following example calculates the standard deviation of the aircraft seats by body style.

```
SELECT act_body_style, act_seats,
       STDDEV(act_seats) OVER (PARTITION BY act_body_style)
STDV_BY_STYLE
FROM   aircraft_types;
```

```
ACT_BODY_STYLE  ACT_SEATS STDV_BY_STYLE
--------------  --------- -------------
Narrow                240    23.0940108
Narrow                200    23.0940108
Narrow                200    23.0940108
Wide                  525    85.4967836
Wide                  407    85.4967836
Wide                  296    85.4967836
Wide                  350    85.4967836
Wide                  416    85.4967836
```

## LAG

This function allows a query to access more than one row of a table simultaneously without performing a self join. LAG provides access to a row at a given physical offset prior to the current row. LAG takes two optional arguments, an offset and a default value. The offset argument, if specified, should be an integer greater than zero (the default is 1). The default value will be returned if the offset goes beyond the scope of the window (by default this is NULL). The following example uses LAG with an offset of two and no default value set. The first two rows are outside the scope and return NULL. The remaining rows return the ACT_SEATS value from two rows prior.

```
SELECT act_body_style, act_seats,
       LAG(act_seats, 2) OVER (ORDER BY act_seats) LAG_BY_STYLE
FROM   aircraft_types;

ACT_BODY_STYLE  ACT_SEATS LAG_BY_STYLE
--------------  --------- ------------
Narrow                200
Narrow                200
Narrow                240          200
Wide                  296          200
Wide                  350          240
Wide                  407          296
Wide                  416          350
Wide                  525          407
```

## LEAD

This is the counterpart to LAG and allows a query to access rows following the current one. The arguments and defaults are the same as those of LAG.

```
SELECT act_body_style, act_seats,
       LEAD(act_seats, 1, 0) OVER (ORDER BY act_seats) LEAD_BY_STYLE
FROM   aircraft_types;

ACT_BODY_STYLE  ACT_SEATS LEAD_BY_STYLE
-------------- ---------- -------------
Narrow                200           200
Narrow                200           240
Narrow                240           296
Wide                  296           350
Wide                  350           407
Wide                  407           416
Wide                  416           525
Wide                  525             0
```

LISTAGG

For a specified measure, LISTAGG orders data within each group specified in the ORDER BY clause and then concatenates the values of the measure column.

- As a single-set aggregate function, LISTAGG operates on all rows and returns a single output row.
- As a group-set aggregate, the function operates on and returns an output row for each group defined by the GROUP BY clause.
- As an analytic function, LISTAGG partitions the query result set into groups based on one or more expression in the query_partition_clause.

```
SELECT LISTAGG(act_name, ': ')
         WITHIN GROUP (ORDER BY act_seats, act_name) AIRCRAFT
  FROM  aircraft_types
  WHERE act_decks = 'Single';

AIRCRAFT
------------------------------------------------------------
Boeing 737: Boeing 757: Boeing 787: Boeing 767: Boeing 777
```

# Using Conversion Functions and Conditional Expressions

## Describe various types of conversion functions that are available in SQL

From what's been presented so far, it's clear that the separation between data types isn't always as complete as it would appear at first glance. For example, dates are stored as a number and can have arithmetic performed on them but are always displayed as character data. For this reason, it's an extremely common occurrence for the Oracle server to receive data in one data type when it expects a different one. When that happens, there must be a conversion operation.

**Implicit Conversion**

Any time a SQL operation encounters an argument of a data type other than the one expected, Oracle will make an attempt to convert the argument to the expected type. If the conversion is successful, then Oracle will perform the SQL function with no outward indication that the conversion took place. If the conversion is unsuccessful, the operation will fail, and an error will be generated.

This automatic process is called implicit conversion. Oracle is so good at implicit conversion that the only time you realize that a conversion operation is taking place is when something prevents it from doing so and you get an error.

The implicit conversion of number to character and Oracle stored date values to character is seamless and the conversion itself will never generate errors. Any number value can also be a character value. Returned date values will always be implicitly converted to a character format matching the current NLS_DATE_FORMAT parameter (or the default of 'DD-MON-YY' if that parameter isn't set).

Implicit conversion of character to number only works when the character is a valid number. Implicitly converting '2354' to number will succeed whereas implicitly converting '14a', '2,423', or '$12.52' will fail because non-numeric elements are present in the character string. Likewise converting a character to a date implicitly will succeed only if the character data matches the current NLS_DATE_FORMAT parameter. If there is anything that prevents an implicit conversion from taking place, you must explicitly convert the data.

In the following example, the NLS_DATE_FORMAT is DD-MON-RR and so Oracle is able to implicitly convert the character data '01-MAY-03' into a date and execute the query.

```
SELECT emp_first, emp_last, emp_job, start_date
FROM   employees
WHERE  start_date > '01-MAY-03';

EMP_FIRST  EMP_LAST   EMP_JOB    START_DATE
---------- ---------- ---------- ----------
Dell       Aptop      Pilot      22-AUG-03
Noh        Kia        Pilot      07-JUL-04
```

Executing the query using a different date format generates an error because implicit date conversion fails:

```
SELECT emp_first, emp_last, emp_job, start_date
FROM   employees
WHERE  start_date > '01-05-03';

SQL Error: ORA-01843: not a valid month
01843. 00000 -  "not a valid month"
```

**Explicit Conversion**

Despite how good Oracle is at implicit conversion, it's not really good practice to rely on it. When implicit conversion fails, it generates errors and stops whatever process was being performed. The recommended practice is that you use the available functions where there is a need to convert data from one data type into the required data type. This is known as explicit conversion. The three most common conversion functions are:

- **TO_CHAR** – Converts a number or date value into a character data type.
- **TO_NUMBER** – Converts a character string into a number data type.
- **TO_DATE** – Converts a character or number data type into a date data type.

There are other conversion functions – notably some involving LOB or Large Object data types. However, you are very unlikely to see these on the exam. To learn more about them, you should make use of the Oracle SQL Reference Manual.

Explicitly converting the date from the previous example allows the query to execute successfully:

```
SELECT emp_first, emp_last, emp_job, start_date
FROM   employees
WHERE  start_date > TO_DATE('01-05-03', 'DD-MM-YY');

EMP_FIRST  EMP_LAST   EMP_JOB    START_DATE
---------- ---------- ---------- ----------
Dell       Aptop      Pilot      22-AUG-03
Noh        Kia        Pilot      07-JUL-04
```

## Use the TO_CHAR, TO_NUMBER, and TO_DATE conversion functions

### Using the TO_CHAR function

The TO_CHAR function has three variants depending on the input data type: TO_CHAR (character), TO_CHAR(datetime), and TO_CHAR(number). The first of the three is used to convert multibyte characters or CLOB data to a VARCHAR2 data type. It is the least commonly seen and is unlikely to be represented on the test. This guide will deal with the second two variants.

**TO_CHAR**

**Syntax:** TO_CHAR(datetime, 'fmt', 'nlsparam')

**Purpose:** TO_CHAR (datetime) converts a datetime or interval value of DATE, TIMESTAMP, TIMESTAMP WITH TIME ZONE, TIMESTAMP WITH LOCAL TIME ZONE, INTERVAL DAY TO SECOND, or INTERVAL YEAR TO MONTH data type to a value of VARCHAR2 data type in the format specified by the date format fmt.

The following example demonstrates converting (and splitting) the system date into separate date and time values.

```
SELECT TO_CHAR(SYSDATE, 'YYYY, MON DD') AS TC_DATE,
       TO_CHAR(SYSDATE, 'HH:MI AM') AS TC_TIME
FROM   dual;

TC_DATE               TC_TIME
--------------------- --------
2012, APR 07          11:23 PM
```

**TO_CHAR**

**Syntax:** TO_CHAR(n, 'fmt', 'nlsparam')

**Purpose:** TO_CHAR (number) converts n to a value of VARCHAR2 data type, using the optional number format fmt. If you omit fmt, then n is converted to a VARCHAR2 value exactly long enough to hold its significant digits. When the nlsparam value is specified, it determines the decimal character, group separator, local currency symbol, and the international currency symbol of the returned value.

```
SELECT TO_CHAR('4235.34','FML9,999.99') "To_char_Ex"
FROM   dual;

To_char_Ex
--------------------
$4,235.34
```

### Using the TO_NUMBER function

The TO_NUMBER function of Oracle is generally used when you have numeric data that is currently in a character data type and you need to perform arithmetic on it, pass it to a function expecting a numeric argument, or store it in a NUMBER field of a table. Oracle's implicit conversion works extremely well when character data is already formatted as a bare number. The most common use of TO_NUMBER is when the character string contains non-numeric aspects. This might be dollar signs, commas, or other formatting elements that will prevent Oracle from being able to determine the specific numeric value to convert the string to.

### TO_NUMBER

**Syntax:** TO_NUMBER(expr, fmt, 'nlsparam')

**Purpose:** Converts *expr* to a value of NUMBER data type. The *expr* can be a BINARY_DOUBLE value or a character data type containing a number in the format specified by the optional format model *fmt*. The optional 'nlsparam' argument specifies the language of the char input.

```
SELECT TO_NUMBER('$4,235.34','FML9,999.99') "To_number_Ex"
FROM   dual;

To_number_Ex
------------
4235.34
```

```
SELECT TO_NUMBER('3.4E+05', '9.9EEEE')
FROM   dual;

TO_NUMBER('3.4E+05','9.9EEEE')
------------------------------
                        340000
```

## Using the TO_DATE Function

As with the TO_NUMBER function, you are required to use the TO_DATE conversion function when a character value is in a date format that Oracle does not recognize implicitly. The default date format that Oracle uses is dependent on options chosen during the install. One of the more common default formats is DD-MON-YY. This default can be altered by setting the parameter NLS_DATE_FORMAT for either the session or the database. The TO_DATE function, however, can be used to convert text to a date from any format that can be expressed with a date format string. The date format strings in Oracle are flexible enough that this evaluates to effectively any date format.

## TO_DATE

**Syntax:** TO_DATE(char, fmt, 'nlsparam')

**Purpose:** Converts character data to a value of DATE data type. fmt is a datetime model format matching the char input. If fmt is omitted, char must be in the default date format. The optional 'nlsparam' argument specifies the language of the char input.

```
SELECT TO_DATE('February 23, 2012, 2:23 P.M.', 'Month dd, YYYY, HH:MI
A.M.') AS "To_date_Ex"
FROM   dual;

To_date_Ex
----------
23-FEB-12
```

Most of the conversion formats from character to date are alphanumeric. The exception is a Julian date. When using TO_DATE to convert a Julian date, the char value must evaluate to an integer value. The integer can be enclosed in single quotes or not.

```
SELECT TO_DATE(2456029, 'J') AS "To_date_Ex"
FROM   dual;

To_date_Ex
----------
11-APR-12
```

### Format Modifiiers

The fx format modifier alters the behavior of Oracle's format checking when it is included as part of the format model. FX stands for 'format exact' and forces the character data being checked to match exactly with the supplied format model. Using one of the previous examples, an extra space is added in the string to be converted before '2012'. The original format model supplied in that example is still able to recognize and convert the date.

```
SELECT TO_DATE('February 23,  2012, 2:23 P.M.', 'Month dd, YYYY,
HH:MI A.M.') AS "To_date_Ex"
FROM   dual;

To_date_Ex
----------
23-FEB-12
```

However, when the 'fx' modifier is placed in front of the format model and the statement executed again, the conversion fails because the format model expects only a single space between the comma and year.

```
SELECT TO_DATE('February 23,  2012, 2:23 P.M.',
               'fxMonth dd, YYYY, HH:MI A.M.') AS "To_date_Ex"
FROM   dual;
```

```
SQL Error: ORA-01841: (full) year must be between -4713 and +9999,
and not be 0
01841. 00000 -  "(full) year must be between -4713 and +9999, and not
be 0"
*Cause:    Illegal year entered
*Action:   Input year in the specified range
```

A second modifier available to format models is fm which stands for 'Fill Mode'. By default Oracle fills format elements converted via the TO_CHAR function to a constant width using trailing blanks for character models and leading zeroes for numeric models. The width used is equal to the display width of the largest relevant format model element. For example, when using TO_CHAR to format a date value using the MONTH model when the date language is AMERICAN, the longest month name is 'September' so all months are right-padded to nine characters. The format model HH24 is left-padded to two digits with a '0'. The fm modifier is used to toggle that padding off or on. The first time it is used in a format model, the padding will be turned off. If it appears a second time, the padding will be turned back on. For example, the two queries below demonstrate the results with and without the fm modifier:

```
SELECT TO_CHAR(SYSDATE, 'MONTH DD  HH24:MI') AS no_fm
FROM dual;

JULY      13  09:50

SELECT TO_CHAR(SYSDATE, 'fmMONTH DD HH24:MI') AS no_fm
FROM dual;

JULY 13 9:50
```

Note that using the fm modifier a second time in the same model turns the fill mode back on:

```
SELECT TO_CHAR(SYSDATE, 'fmMONTH DD fmHH24:MI') AS no_fm
FROM dual;

JULY 13 09:50
```

## Apply general functions and conditional expressions in a SELECT statement

Conditional expressions provide SQL statements with the ability to perform IF-THEN-ELSE decisions. This is a very useful capability as it gives SQL a small portion of the procedural capabilities that otherwise would require a PL/SQL block. The two conditional expressions that can be performed within SQL in Oracle are CASE and DECODE. The CASE function is part of the capabilities defined within the ANSI SQL specification whereas DECODE is an Oracle-proprietary function. As a general rule, using ANSI SQL is considered better practice, so it is the conditional expression that I would recommend using and the one more likely to appear on an exam question.

The syntax for a CASE statement is:

```
CASE expr
    WHEN comp_1 THEN return_1;
    [WHEN comp_2 THEN return_2, …]
    ELSE return_else
END CASE;
```

In processing a CASE statement, Oracle will evaluate the WHEN conditions from top-down. As soon as any of the conditions evaluates to TRUE, the evaluation process stops and the value listed in the current WHEN condition is returned by the CASE statement. If none of the WHEN conditions evaluates to TRUE, the value in the ELSE condition is returned by the CASE statement. If a CASE statement doesn't match any of the supplied WHEN conditions and no ELSE condition is provided, Oracle will return NULL. The following CASE example provides a return value that depends on the employee's job title.

```
SELECT emp_first || ' ' || emp_last,
       CASE emp_job
         WHEN 'CEO' THEN 'This is the big Kahuna'
         WHEN 'CFO' THEN 'The dude holding the piggy bank'
         WHEN 'SVP' THEN 'Senior right-hand guy'
         WHEN 'VP' THEN 'Right-hand guy'
         WHEN 'SrDir' THEN 'Middle Management'
         WHEN 'Mgr' THEN 'Lower Management'
         ELSE 'Just another peon'
       END CASE
FROM   employees
ORDER BY emp_id;

EMP_FIRST||''||EMP_LAST CASE
----------------------- -------------------------------
Big Boss                This is the big Kahuna
Adam Smith              The dude holding the piggy bank
Rick Jameson            Senior right-hand guy
Rob Stoner              Senior right-hand guy
Bill Abong              Right-hand guy
Janet Jeckson           Right-hand guy
Fred Stoneflint         Middle Management
Alf Alien               Middle Management
Norm Storm              Lower Management
John Jones              Just another peon
Top Gun                 Just another peon
Phil McCoy              Just another peon
James Thomas            Just another peon
John Picard             Just another peon
Luke Skytalker          Just another peon
Dell Aptop              Just another peon
Noh Kia                 Just another peon
```

When creating a CASE statement, the conditions must be given careful consideration. The example below has two flaws that affect the results for the 747 and 757. There is no condition that covers planes with 220-250 seats, so nothing is returned for the 757. The second problem is that the 747 should class as a 'Jumbo Airplane' based on the conditions. However, since conditions are evaluated from the top down, the 747 meets the criteria for the 'Bigger Airplane' and later conditions are not evaluated.

```
SELECT act_name, act_seats,
       CASE
         WHEN act_seats < 220 THEN 'Small Airplane'
         WHEN act_seats > 250 THEN 'Bigger Airplane'
         WHEN act_seats > 400 THEN 'Jumbo Airplane'
       END CASE
FROM   aircraft_types;

ACT_NAME     ACT_SEATS CASE
------------ --------- ---------------
Boeing 747         416 Bigger Airplane
Boeing 767         350 Bigger Airplane
Boeing 737         200 Small Airplane
Boeing 757         240
```

The DECODE statement predates Oracle's implementation of the CASE capability. It provides a similar capability to CASE, but is not quite as flexible. It is designed to evaluate equality only, whereas CASE can use multiple conditional operators (>, <, !=, etc.) In addition, when a DECODE statement is evaluating multiple conditions, it becomes difficult to read. The syntax for DECODE is:

```
DECODE(expr, search, result [,search2, result2…], default)
```

A DECODE function compares the value of expr to each search value one by one. If expr is equal to a search value, then processing stops and the function returns the corresponding result. If no match is found, the default is returned. If there is no default, then the DECODE returns null. All of those are identical to the behavior of a CASE except the last.

```
SELECT apt_name,
       DECODE(apt_abbr,
              'MCO', 'Going to Disneyworld',
              'MIA', 'CSI Miami, here I come',
              'ATL', 'Need to get some peaches',
              'DFW', 'Everything is bigger in Texas',
              'Is Jacksonville known for anything?')
           AS DC_RETVAL
FROM   airports;
```

```
APT_NAME           DC_RETVAL
------------------ -------------------------------------
Orlando, FL        Going to Disneyworld
Atlanta, GA        Need to get some peaches
Miami, FL          CSI Miami, here I come
Jacksonville, FL   Is Jacksonville known for anything?
Dallas/Fort Worth  Everything is bigger in Texas
```

# Reporting Aggregated Data Using the Group Functions

## Describe the use of group functions

Group functions (also known as aggregate functions) act against one or more rows and return a single result. This is in comparison to single-row functions that always return one result for each row processed by a given query. Aggregate functions are useful for analyzing data across multiple rows and for generating data that applies to one or more sets of rows (like the highest salary or the average age). The data returned might be in multiple groups based on column data if the SELECT statement contains a GROUP BY clause.

As with the Oracle SQL functions, there are too many group functions available to define them all in this guide. Some of the more common ones follow. For a complete list, you should refer to the SQL Language Reference manual.

**AVG**

**Syntax:** AVG(DISTINCT/ALL *expr*)

**Purpose:** AVG returns average value of *expr*.

```
SELECT AVG(salary) "Average"
FROM   employees;

Average
-------
115814.70588235294117647058823529411764 71
```

**COUNT**

**Syntax:** COUNT(DISTINCT/ALL *expr*)

**Purpose:** COUNT returns the number of rows where *expr* has at least one non-NULL value.

```
SELECT COUNT(emp_id) "NoNullCount",
       COUNT(afl_id) "CountHasNulls"
FROM   employees;

NoNullCount CountHasNulls
----------- -------------
         17             8
```

The above example demonstrates that the COUNT function will not count individual columns when they contain a NULL value. However, COUNT(*) will count all rows that meet the filter condition even if every single column value is NULL. This is demonstrated with the below example:

```
CREATE TABLE count_null_test (
col1        VARCHAR2(1),
col2        VARCHAR2(1)
);
table COUNT_NULL_TEST created.

INSERT INTO count_null_test VALUES (NULL, NULL);
1 rows inserted.
INSERT INTO count_null_test VALUES (NULL, NULL);
1 rows inserted.
INSERT INTO count_null_test VALUES (NULL, NULL);
1 rows inserted.


SELECT COUNT(*), COUNT(col1), COUNT(col2)
FROM   count_null_test;

COUNT(*) COUNT(COL1) COUNT(COL2)
-------- ----------- -----------
       3           0           0
```

### MEDIAN

**Syntax:** MEDIAN(*expr*)

**Purpose:** MEDIAN takes a numeric or datetime value and returns the middle value or an interpolated value that would be the middle value once the values are sorted.

```
SELECT emp_job, MEDIAN(salary)
FROM employees
GROUP BY emp_job
ORDER BY MEDIAN(salary) DESC;

EMP_JOB                         MEDIAN(SALARY)
------------------------------ --------------
CEO                                    197500
CFO                                    157000
SVP                                    147150
VP                                     125650
SrDir                                  111000
Mgr                                    101500
Pilot                                   92875
```

## MIN

**Syntax:** MIN(DISTINCT/ALL *expr*)

**Purpose:** MIN returns minimum value of *expr*.

```
SELECT MIN(start_date) "Earliest"
FROM   employees;

Earliest
---------
10-APR-92
```

## MAX

**Syntax:** MAX(DISTINCT/ALL *expr*)

**Purpose:** MAX returns the maximum value of *expr*.

```
SELECT MAX(start_date) "Latest"
FROM   employees;

Latest
---------
07-JUL-04
```

## SUM

**Syntax:** SUM(DISTINCT/ALL *expr*)

**Purpose:** SUM returns the sum of all expr values.

```
SELECT SUM(salary) "Sum_Salary"
FROM   employees;

Sum_Salary
----------
   1935350
```

Aggregate functions are intended to group together multiple rows based on a supplied common factor and return a single result for the entire group rather than one result for each row in the table. These functions can appear in select lists and in ORDER BY and HAVING clauses. Aggregate functions are not allowed in a WHERE clause:

Aggregates are commonly used in conjunction with the GROUP BY clause in a SELECT statement. When a query contains a GROUP BY clause, the individual elements of the select list can be aggregate functions, GROUP BY expressions, constants, or expressions involving one of these. The aggregate functions will be applied to each group of rows and a single result row returned for each group.

```
SELECT emp_job, MAX(salary)
FROM   employees
GROUP BY emp_job;

EMP_JOB    MAX(SALARY)
---------- -----------
VP              127800
SrDir           111500
SVP             149100
Mgr             101500
Pilot           105000
CEO             197500
CFO             157000
```

When a query contains aggregate functions but no GROUP BY clause, the aggregate functions in the select list are applied to all the rows returned by the query. In this event, one row would be returned for the entire statement.

```
SELECT MAX(salary)
FROM   employees;

MAX(SALARY)
-----------
     197500
```

Many aggregate functions that take a single argument will accept the use of the DISTINCT/UNIQUE keyword. These will cause an aggregate function to consider only distinct values of the argument expression. Aggregate functions that will accept DISTINCT/UNIQUE will also accept the ALL keyword. This causes an aggregate function to consider all values, including all duplicates. If you specify no keyword, then the default is ALL. The first example below uses the ALL keyword and the second does not. The results are identical.

```
SELECT COUNT(DISTINCT emp_job) distinct_values,
       COUNT(ALL emp_job) AS all_values
FROM   employees;

DISTINCT_VALUES ALL_VALUES
--------------- ----------
              7         17
```

```
SELECT COUNT(DISTINCT emp_job) distinct_values,
       COUNT(emp_job) AS all_values
FROM   employees;

DISTINCT_VALUES ALL_VALUES
--------------- ----------
              7         17
```

By default, NULL values are ignored by all of the aggregate functions. There are exceptions to this rule: the COUNT(*) function as described earlier as well as the GROUPING, and GROUPING_ID aggregate functions.

The GROUPING and GROUPING_ID syntax is not listed in the exam topics and should not appear on this exam. If you are asked a question about NULLs and aggregate functions, the answer they are looking for is almost certain to be that they are ignored.

The COUNT function will never return a NULL no matter what the values in the table are. The result of the COUNT function will be an integer value 0 or greater. All other aggregate functions will return a NULL value if a data set either has no rows or has only rows with NULL as the aggregate function argument.

Not all of the aggregate functions can be used against all data types.

- AVG, SUM, MIN, and MAX can be used against numeric data
- MIN and MAX can be used against date and character data as well
- COUNT can be used against essentially any data

Below, the MAX function is used successfully against date and character data. Recall from earlier, however, that character-based sorting (and therefore the 'highest' and 'lowest') values are not necessarily what you would expect. The 'MAX' value of a character field that included '3', '12', and '1000000' would be '3'.

```
SELECT MAX(emp_first) AS "Max_First",
       MAX(start_date) AS "Max_Start"
FROM   employees;

Max_First  Max_Start
---------- ---------
Top        07-JUL-04
```

If you try to use an aggregate function on a data type that is not supported, you will receive an error. It might seem like pulling the average from a set of dates would be reasonable, but this is not possible using AVG:

```
SELECT AVG(start_date)
FROM   employees;

SQL Error: ORA-00932: inconsistent datatypes: expected NUMBER got
DATE
00932. 00000 -  "inconsistent datatypes: expected %s got %s"
```

## Group data by using the GROUP BY clause

You specify the GROUP BY clause when you want Oracle to group selected rows based on the value of one or more expressions for each row and return a single row of summary information for each group. Expressions in the GROUP BY clause can contain any columns of the tables in the FROM clause, regardless of whether the columns appear in the select list. The GROUP BY clause groups rows but it does not guarantee the order of the result set. You must make use of the ORDER BY clause to order the grouped results. When a SELECT clause contains one or more aggregate functions, any column that is not included in a group function must be part of the GROUP BY clause.

```
SELECT emp_job, MAX(salary) max_salary
FROM   employees
GROUP BY emp_job;

EMP_JOB                        MAX_SALARY
------------------------------ ----------
VP                                 127800
SrDir                              111500
SVP                                149100
Mgr                                101500
Pilot                               98500
CEO                                197500
CFO                                157000
```

```
SELECT emp_job, MAX(salary) max_salary
FROM   employees
GROUP BY emp_job
ORDER BY emp_job;
```

```
EMP_JOB                        MAX_SALARY
------------------------------ ----------
CEO                                197500
CFO                                157000
Mgr                                101500
Pilot                               98500
SVP                                149100
SrDir                              111500
VP                                 127800
```

When you add additional columns to a GROUP BY clause, you will (generally) increase the number of groups returned by the query. The below examples show data from the AIRCRAFT_FLEET_V view grouped by one column, and then by two columns.

```
SELECT apt_name, SUM(act_seats)
FROM   aircraft_fleet_v
GROUP BY apt_name;

APT_NAME               SUM(ACT_SEATS)
---------------------- --------------
Miami, FL                         832
Atlanta, GA                       440
Orlando, FL                       700
Dallas/Fort Worth                 766
```

```
SELECT apt_name, act_name, SUM(act_seats)
FROM   aircraft_fleet_v
GROUP BY apt_name, act_name;

APT_NAME               ACT_NAME     SUM(ACT_SEATS)
---------------------- ------------ --------------
Atlanta, GA            Boeing 757              240
Dallas/Fort Worth      Boeing 767              350
Orlando, FL            Boeing 767              700
Atlanta, GA            Boeing 737              200
Miami, FL              Boeing 747              832
Dallas/Fort Worth      Boeing 747              416
```

Grouping functions can be nested within another grouping function to a limited degree. It is possible to nest two levels of grouped functions, but not three. When nesting aggregate functions, the GROUP BY clause is mandatory. In the example below, the average number of seats grouped by the number of decks is calculated.

```
SELECT AVG(act_seats)
FROM   aircraft_types
GROUP BY act_decks;

AVG(ACT_SEATS)
--------------
263.3333333333
           416
```

The SQL from the above query is modified to generate the maximum of the average values returned and completes successfully:

```
SELECT MAX(AVG(act_seats))
FROM   aircraft_types
GROUP BY act_decks;

MAX(AVG(ACT_SEATS))
-------------------
                416
```

The following example attempts to add one more level of nesting and generates an ORA-00935 error:

```
SELECT COUNT(MAX(AVG(act_seats)))
FROM   aircraft_types
GROUP BY act_decks;

SQL Error: ORA-00935: group function is nested too deeply
00935. 00000 -  "group function is nested too deeply"
*Cause:
*Action:
```

An error is also returned if the nesting SQL does not include a GROUP BY clause:

```
SELECT MAX(AVG(act_seats))
FROM   aircraft_types;

SQL Error: ORA-00978: nested group function without GROUP BY
00978. 00000 -  "nested group function without GROUP BY"
```

## Include or exclude grouped rows by using the HAVING clause

When the GROUP BY clause is present in a SQL statement, you can also make use of the HAVING clause. The HAVING clause is used to restrict the groups of returned rows to those groups for which the specified condition is TRUE. If the HAVING clause is omitted, then the database returns summary rows for all groups generated by the query. The GROUP BY and HAVING clauses must be after the WHERE clause and hierarchical query clause (hierarchical queries are discussed later in this guide), but before the ORDER BY clause. If you specify both GROUP BY and HAVING, then they can appear in either order. If a HAVING clause contains a subquery, the subquery is resolved before evaluating the HAVING clause.

The WHERE clause is evaluated before the data is aggregated by a query. Therefore, any conditions in the WHERE clause will remove individual rows prior to the aggregation. You should always keep in mind that WHERE conditions apply to rows and HAVING conditions apply to groups. Aggregate functions cannot be referenced in the WHERE clause and the HAVING clause cannot filter individual rows.

We'll add another filter to the above query to remove the CEO from the results by adding a second condition to the HAVING clause. Since the CEO is a single row in the table, you might expect this to generate an error. However it succeeds and returns the expected results.

```
SELECT emp_job, MAX(salary) max_salary
FROM   employees
GROUP BY emp_job
HAVING MAX(salary) > 111500
AND    emp_job != 'CEO'
ORDER BY emp_job;

EMP_JOB    MAX_SALARY
---------- ----------
CFO            157000
SVP            149100
VP             127800
```

Filtering the CEO using the WHERE clause also works:

```
SELECT emp_job, MAX(salary) max_salary
FROM   employees
WHERE  emp_job != 'CEO'
GROUP BY emp_job
HAVING MAX(salary) > 111500
ORDER BY emp_job;

EMP_JOB    MAX_SALARY
---------- ----------
CFO            157000
SVP            149100
VP             127800
```

The reason why this works in either the WHERE or HAVING clauses is because EMP_JOB is part of the GROUP BY clause. Even though only a single row evaluates to 'CEO', the HAVING filter is still removing an entire group. If the HAVING filter were changed to "emp_last != 'Boss'" (which evaluates to the same row in the table), the SELECT statement fails with an error:

```
SELECT emp_job, MAX(salary) max_salary
FROM   employees
GROUP BY emp_job
HAVING MAX(salary) > 111500
AND    emp_last != 'Boss'
ORDER BY emp_job;

SQL Error: ORA-00979: not a GROUP BY expression
00979. 00000 -  "not a GROUP BY expression"
*Cause:
*Action:
```

When filtering by columns that are not part of the SELECT list, you must use a condition in the WHERE clause:

```
SELECT emp_job, MAX(salary) max_salary
FROM   employees
WHERE  emp_last != 'Boss'
GROUP BY emp_job
HAVING MAX(salary) > 111500
ORDER BY emp_job;
```

```
EMP_JOB    MAX_SALARY
---------- ----------
CFO            157000
SVP            149100
VP             127800
```

# Displaying Data from Multiple Tables

## Describe the different types of joins and their features

Any query that combines rows from two or more tables, views, materialized views, subqueries, or table functions must make use of joins (henceforth I'll use the word 'table' to mean any of these). Oracle will perform a join operation any time multiple tables appear in the FROM clause of the query. When multiple tables exist in the FROM clause, the select list can include any combination of columns from any of the tables. When more than one table has a column name in common, then references to duplicated columns must be qualified in all parts of the query (with the exception of join columns in NATURAL or JOIN USING joins). You qualify a column name by prefixing it with the table name followed by a period, or with the table alias followed by a period.

The following example joins three tables together: AIRPORTS, AIRCRAFT_FLEET and AIRCRAFT_TYPES. Connecting the three tables requires two join operations. First AIRPORTS is joined to the AIRCRAFT_FLEET table using the APT_ID column that exists in both tables. Second, the AIRCRAFT_FLEET table is joined to the AIRCRAFT_TYPES table by the ACT_ID column that exists in both tables. The AIRPORTS and AIRCRAFT_TYPES tables are not directly joined. The connection between these two tables is through the AIRCRAFT_FLEET table that both are joined to.

```
SELECT apt_name, apt_abbr, act_name, act_seats
FROM   airports apt
       INNER JOIN aircraft_fleet afl
       ON apt.apt_id = afl.apt_id
       INNER JOIN aircraft_types act
       ON act.act_id = afl.act_id;
```

```
APT_NAME            APT_ABBR ACT_NAME     ACT_SEATS
------------------- -------- ------------ ---------
Orlando, FL         MCO      Boeing 767         350
Orlando, FL         MCO      Boeing 767         350
Atlanta, GA         ATL      Boeing 757         240
Atlanta, GA         ATL      Boeing 737         200
Miami, FL           MIA      Boeing 747         416
Miami, FL           MIA      Boeing 747         416
Dallas/Fort Worth   DFW      Boeing 767         350
Dallas/Fort Worth   DFW      Boeing 747         416
```

Prior to release 9i, Oracle exclusively used a proprietary join format for connecting tables. With the release of 9i, Oracle began supporting the ANSI standard (SQL:1999) join format as well. As a general rule, people simply refer to this as "ANSI SQL". The ANSI style has no performance benefits over the proprietary format. SQL written using ANSI style joins are generally a bit more readable and offer more options when specifying OUTER joins between tables. The ANSI format is the preferred style per Oracle and is what you should see on the test in any questions containing joins. It is always possible that the test developers might include one or more queries that utilize the proprietary format, though.

The syntax for a join operation using SQL:1999 syntax is:

```
SELECT t1.*, t2.*
FROM   table1 t1
       [NATURAL JOIN table2 t2] |
       [JOIN table2 t2 USING (col_name)] |
       [INNER JOIN table2 t2
        ON (t1.col1 = t2.col2)] |
       [LEFT|RIGHT|FULL OUTER JOIN table2 t2
        ON (t1.col1 = t2.col2)] |
       [CROSS JOIN table2 t2];
```

You should understand the various join definitions.

- **EQUIJOIN** -- A join where the condition contains an equality operator. An equijoin combines rows that have equivalent values for the specified columns.
- **NON-EQUIJOIN** -- A join where the condition does not contain an equality operator – (e.g. the operator might be greater than or

less than). A non-equijoin combines rows that have non-equivalent values for the specified columns.

- **SELF-JOIN** -- A join of a table back to itself. The given table will appear twice (or more) in the FROM clause. All incarnations should have table aliases to allow you to qualify column names in the join condition and other parts of the query.
- **INNER JOIN --** An inner join (sometimes called a simple join) is a join of two or more tables that returns only those rows that satisfy the join condition.
- **FULL OUTER JOIN --** An outer join returns all rows that satisfy the join condition and also returns all of those rows from the tables for which no rows from the other satisfy the join condition.
- **LEFT OUTER JOIN –** A left join is a subset of the outer join where all of the rows in the table on the left-side in the FROM clause are returned and only the rows that meet the join condition are returned from the table on the right side in the FROM clause.
- **RIGHT OUTER JOIN –** A right join is the opposite of the left join. All of the rows in the table identified on the right-side in the FROM clause are returned and only the rows that meet the join condition are returned from the table on the left side in the FROM clause.
- **CROSS JOIN** -- A cross join is the result when two tables are included in a query but no join condition is specified. When this is the case, Oracle returns the Cartesian product of the two tables (this is sometimes called a Cartesian Join). The Cartesian product is when every row of one table is joined with every row of the other. Generally considered to be useless, cross joins are most often created by mistake.
- **NATURAL JOIN –** A natural join can only be used when the column names and data types used for the join match in both tables. It will perform an inner-equijoin between the two tables.

Note that the above definitions are not exclusive. A join will often fulfill more than one of these definitions at a time. For example, a natural join is always an equijoin and an inner join. A self join is probably an equijoin an inner join as well.

## Use SELECT statements to access data from more than one table using equijoins and nonequijoins

When performing a SELECT operation against a single table, there is never any question of what table a given column name in the query belongs to. When multiple tables are joined together, however, it's possible for a query to reference a column name that exists in more than one of the joined tables. When this happens, Oracle must have a means of identifying the correct column. The method by which this is done is called qualifying the column. The table name or table alias is placed in front of the column name followed by a period (i.e. table_name.column_name or table_alias.column_name). It is not required to prefix columns where the table name can be determined by the Oracle SQL parser, but doing so makes the SQL more readable and provides a slight performance improvement during the parse operation.

When a table has been aliased in a query, it is not legal to use the table name as a prefix – you must use the alias. Using the table name will generate an error.

```
SELECT airports.apt_name, airports.apt_abbr
FROM   airports ap;

SQL Error: ORA-00904: "AIRPORTS"."APT_ABBR": invalid identifier
00904. 00000 -  "%s: invalid identifier"
*Cause:
*Action:
```

If the table is given no alias, then using the full name for a column prefix is legal (and the only way to qualify the column):

```
SELECT airports.apt_name, airports.apt_abbr
FROM   airports;

APT_NAME               APT_ABBR
---------------------- --------
Orlando, FL            MCO
Atlanta, GA            ATL
Miami, FL              MIA
Jacksonville, FL       JAX
Dallas/Fort Worth      DFW
```

If the table is given an alias, then you must use the alias as a column prefix or no prefix at all:

```
SELECT apt.apt_name, apt_abbr
FROM   airports apt;

APT_NAME                 APT_ABBR
----------------------   --------
Orlando, FL              MCO
Atlanta, GA              ATL
Miami, FL                MIA
Jacksonville, FL         JAX
Dallas/Fort Worth        DFW
```

**Equijoins**

The vast majority of JOIN operations use equijoins. In an equijoin there is a condition such that column A in table one EQUALS column B in table two. As a general rule, when there's a need to join two tables, it will be by column data that is exactly equal. The below query uses three equijoins and connects four tables together to generate the required results.

```
SELECT apt_name, act_name, emp_first, emp_last
FROM   airports apt
       INNER JOIN aircraft_fleet afl
       ON apt.apt_id = afl.apt_id
       INNER JOIN aircraft_types act
       ON act.act_id = afl.act_id
       INNER JOIN employees emp
       ON afl.afl_id = emp.afl_id;

APT_NAME                ACT_NAME      EMP_FIRST    EMP_LAST
--------------------    ------------  -----------  --------------
Orlando, FL             Boeing 767    John         Jones
Orlando, FL             Boeing 767    Top          Gun
Atlanta, GA             Boeing 737    Phil         McCoy
Atlanta, GA             Boeing 757    James        Thomas
Miami, FL               Boeing 747    John         Picard
Miami, FL               Boeing 747    Luke         Skytalker
Dallas/Fort Worth       Boeing 747    Dell         Aptop
Dallas/Fort Worth       Boeing 767    Noh          Kia
```

Because the joins in the above example all are equijoins where the column names match in both tables, the NATURAL JOIN could have been used to generate the same result. If the join column(s) for a NATURAL JOIN are included anywhere else in the query, they should not be qualified with the table name or alias. Many SQL developers (myself included) prefer not to make use of the NATURAL JOIN syntax. When this type of join is used, the join column(s) being used to connect the two tables is not obvious without looking at the table structure. It is also possible to get unexpected results when join being made is not what the developer anticipated. Without looking at the SQL execution plan or performing detailed analysis of the rows returned, this can go unnoticed and generate erroneous data.

```
SELECT apt_name, act_name, emp_first, emp_last
FROM   airports apt
       NATURAL JOIN aircraft_fleet afl
       NATURAL JOIN aircraft_types act
       NATURAL JOIN employees emp;

APT_NAME             ACT_NAME     EMP_FIRST   EMP_LAST
-------------------- ------------ ----------- --------------
Orlando, FL          Boeing 767   John        Jones
Orlando, FL          Boeing 767   Top         Gun
Atlanta, GA          Boeing 737   Phil        McCoy
Atlanta, GA          Boeing 757   James       Thomas
Miami, FL            Boeing 747   John        Picard
Miami, FL            Boeing 747   Luke        Skytalker
Dallas/Fort Worth    Boeing 747   Dell        Aptop
Dallas/Fort Worth    Boeing 767   Noh         Kia
```

A third equivalent option for the query is the JOIN...USING syntax. When the USING clause is utilized, only the column name(s) for the JOIN get specified. JOIN..USING is a more flexible means of performing tables with identical column names than a NATURAL join. Just as with a NATURAL JOIN, it is always an EQUIJOIN and the join column names must always be the same in both tables. However, with JOIN...USING, the columns need not be the exact same data type (i.e. one could be CHAR and another VARCHAR or NCHAR). A NATURAL join between two tables will also join by all columns in the two tables that have matching names. The USING clause can specify a subset of columns with matching names. As with a NATURAL join, if the join column(s) are included anywhere else in the query, they should not be qualified with the table name or alias.

```
SELECT apt_name, act_name, emp_first, emp_last
FROM   airports apt
       JOIN aircraft_fleet afl USING (apt_id)
       JOIN aircraft_types act USING (act_id)
       JOIN employees emp USING (afl_id);

APT_NAME             ACT_NAME     EMP_FIRST   EMP_LAST
-------------------- ------------ ----------- --------------
Orlando, FL          Boeing 767   John        Jones
Orlando, FL          Boeing 767   Top         Gun
Atlanta, GA          Boeing 737   Phil        McCoy
Atlanta, GA          Boeing 757   James       Thomas
Miami, FL            Boeing 747   John        Picard
Miami, FL            Boeing 747   Luke        Skytalker
Dallas/Fort Worth    Boeing 747   Dell        Aptop
Dallas/Fort Worth    Boeing 767   Noh         Kia
```

Finally a fourth syntax option for the query is the JOIN...ON syntax. This is nothing more than the 'INNER JOIN...ON' syntax with the optional 'INNER' left off. However, it's easy to confuse with the JOIN...USING syntax. When the ON syntax is used, the join condition must specify the join columns from both tables (qualified if they are the same name) and the operator. If the join columns are in the SELECT list, they must be qualified with a table name or alias.

```
SELECT apt_name, act_name, emp_first, emp_last
FROM   airports apt
       JOIN aircraft_fleet afl ON (apt.apt_id = afl.apt_id)
       JOIN aircraft_types act ON (afl.act_id = act.act_id)
       JOIN employees emp ON (afl.afl_id = emp.afl_id);

APT_NAME               ACT_NAME     EMP_FIRST  EMP_LAST
---------------------- ------------ ---------- ----------
Orlando, FL            Boeing 767   John       Jones
Orlando, FL            Boeing 767   Top        Gun
Atlanta, GA            Boeing 737   Phil       McCoy
Atlanta, GA            Boeing 757   James      Thomas
Miami, FL              Boeing 747   John       Picard
Miami, FL              Boeing 747   Luke       Skytalker
Dallas/Fort Worth      Boeing 747   Dell       Aptop
Dallas/Fort Worth      Boeing 767   Noh        Kia
```

## NonEquijoins

On occasion, there is a need to perform a non-equijoin. In a non-equijoin, the condition joining the columns of the two tables uses some condition other than EQUALS. In the below example, the EMPLOYEES table is joined to the SALARY_RANGES table. The join operation uses the BETWEEN operator to find which range each employee's salary falls into in order to determine the salary code.

```
SELECT emp.emp_first, emp.emp_last, salary, slr_code
FROM   employees emp
       INNER JOIN salary_ranges slr
       ON emp.salary BETWEEN slr.slr_lowval
                         AND slr.slr_highval
ORDER BY slr_code DESC;

EMP_FIRST    EMP_LAST          SALARY SLR_CODE
------------ ----------------- ------ --------
Big          Boss              197500 S09
Adam         Smith             157000 S07
Rob          Stoner            149100 S07
Rick         Jameson           145200 S07
Janet        Jeckson           127800 S06
Bill         Abong             123500 S06
Norm         Storm             101500 S05
Fred         Stoneflint        111500 S05
Alf          Alien             110500 S05
Luke         Skytalker          90000 S04
Dell         Aptop              87500 S04
Phil         McCoy              93500 S04
Noh          Kia                92250 S04
Top          Gun                91500 S04
John         Picard             94500 S04
James        Thomas             98500 S04
John         Jones              97500 S04
```

## Additional JOIN conditions

You can add additional conditions to the JOIN clause when joining two tables together.

```
SELECT apt_name, act_name, emp_first, emp_last
FROM   airports apt
       JOIN aircraft_fleet afl ON (apt.apt_id = afl.apt_id)
       JOIN aircraft_types act ON (afl.act_id = act.act_id)
                             AND act.act_name='Boeing 767'
       JOIN employees emp ON (afl.afl_id = emp.afl_id);

APT_NAME                ACT_NAME     EMP_FIRST  EMP_LAST
----------------------- ------------ ---------- ----------
Orlando, FL             Boeing 767   John       Jones
Orlando, FL             Boeing 767   Top        Gun
Dallas/Fort Worth       Boeing 767   Noh        Kia
```

With INNER JOINS, the result of adding this condition to the JOIN clause is indistinguishable from adding the same condition to the WHERE clause. Both will produce identical results. For OUTER JOINS, the location of the condition can alter the resulting rows returned.

```
SELECT apt_name, act_name, emp_first, emp_last
FROM   airports apt
       JOIN aircraft_fleet afl ON (apt.apt_id = afl.apt_id)
       JOIN aircraft_types act ON (afl.act_id = act.act_id)
       JOIN employees emp ON (afl.afl_id = emp.afl_id)
WHERE  act.act_name='Boeing 767';

APT_NAME                ACT_NAME     EMP_FIRST  EMP_LAST
----------------------- ------------ ---------- ----------
Orlando, FL             Boeing 767   John       Jones
Orlando, FL             Boeing 767   Top        Gun
Dallas/Fort Worth       Boeing 767   Noh        Kia
```

## Join a table to itself by using a self-join

It's sometimes very useful to join a table back to itself when rows in it reference other rows. In the example below, we join the EMPLOYEES table back to itself by using the EMP_ID and EMP_SUPERVISOR columns. In this fashion we're able to display each employee's manager.

```
SELECT emp.emp_first, emp.emp_last, mgr.emp_first || ' ' ||
mgr.emp_last AS EMP_MANAGER
FROM   employees emp
       LEFT JOIN employees mgr
       ON emp.emp_supervisor = mgr.emp_id
ORDER BY NVL(mgr.emp_supervisor, 0), emp.emp_last, emp.emp_first;
```

```
EMP_FIRST    EMP_LAST        EMP_MANAGER
------------ --------------- --------------
Big          Boss
Rick         Jameson         Big Boss
Adam         Smith           Big Boss
Rob          Stoner          Big Boss
Bill         Abong           Rick Jameson
Janet        Jeckson         Rob Stoner
Fred         Stoneflint      Bill Abong
Alf          Alien           Janet Jeckson
Norm         Storm           Alf Alien
Dell         Aptop           Norm Storm
Top          Gun             Norm Storm
John         Jones           Norm Storm
Noh          Kia             Norm Storm
Phil         McCoy           Norm Storm
John         Picard          Norm Storm
Luke         Skytalker       Norm Storm
James        Thomas          Norm Storm
```

A self join like the above example connects a table back to itself on time. There is a SQL clause called CONNECT BY PRIOR that performs what acts much like multiple self-joins. One of the more common examples of this function is the ability to create organization charts. With the CONNECT BY PRIOR functionality, it is possible to return results that show the chain of an employee to his manager, to his manager's manager, and so forth. The CONNECT BY PRIOR clause is not actually a join operation and will not be on the SQL exam. It is mentioned here to provide a comparison to the way in which a SELF JOIN operation works.

```
SELECT level, emp_first, emp_last, emp_job, emp_id, emp_supervisor
FROM   employees emp
START WITH emp_supervisor IS NULL
CONNECT BY PRIOR emp_id = emp_supervisor;
```

```
LEVEL EMP_FIRST  EMP_LAST   EMP_JOB    EMP_ID EMP_SUPERVISOR
----- ---------- ---------- ---------- ------ --------------
    1 Big        Boss       CEO             1
    2 Adam       Smith      CFO             2              1
    2 Rick       Jameson    SVP             3              1
    3 Bill       Abong      VP              5              3
    4 Fred       Stoneflint SrDir           7              5
    2 Rob        Stoner     SVP             4              1
    3 Janet      Jeckson    VP              6              4
    4 Alf        Alien      SrDir           8              6
    5 Norm       Storm      Mgr             9              8
    6 John       Jones      Pilot          10              9
    6 Top        Gun        Pilot          11              9
    6 Phil       McCoy      Pilot          12              9
    6 James      Thomas     Pilot          13              9
    6 John       Picard     Pilot          14              9
    6 Luke       Skytalker  Pilot          15              9
    6 Dell       Aptop      Pilot          16              9
    6 Noh        Kia        Pilot          17              9
    5 Guy        Newberry   Mgr            18              8
```

## View data that generally does not meet a join condition by using outer joins

When you use an INNER join to link two tables where column A of table one equals column B of table two, any rows from both tables that don't meet the specified condition are not returned by the query. In cases where you would like non-matched rows to be returned, you must use one of the OUTER join syntaxes. There are three varieties of OUTER joins. The behavior of the first two is determined by which side of the join operator a table's column appears on. The definitions below make use of this example: Table1.Column_A = Table2.Column_B

- **LEFT OUTER JOIN** – Rows from the Table1 will be returned regardless of whether or not there are rows in Table2 where Column_A = Column_B. The 'OUTER' portion of the syntax is optional (i.e. 'LEFT OUTER JOIN' and 'LEFT JOIN' are equivalent)
- **RIGHT OUTER JOIN** – Rows from the Table2 will be returned regardless of whether or not there are rows in Table1 where

Column_A = Column_B. The 'OUTER' portion of the syntax is optional (i.e. 'RIGHT OUTER JOIN' and 'RIGHT JOIN' are equivalent)

- **FULL OUTER JOIN** -- Rows from both tables will be returned regardless of whether or not there are rows where Column_A = Column_B.

For the join examples, we'll create the following tables:

```
CREATE TABLE table_A (
  col1      NUMBER,
  col2      VARCHAR2(1)
);

CREATE TABLE table_B (
  col1      NUMBER,
  col2      VARCHAR2(1)
);
```

Now we'll populate them with the below data:

```
INSERT INTO table_A VALUES (1, 'a');
INSERT INTO table_A VALUES (2, 'b');
INSERT INTO table_A VALUES (3, 'c');

INSERT INTO table_B VALUES (2, 'B');
INSERT INTO table_B VALUES (3, 'C');
INSERT INTO table_B VALUES (4, 'D');
```

An INNER JOIN between these two tables produces the following results:

```
SELECT a.col1 AS TA_COL1, a.col2 AS TA_col2,
       b.col1 AS TB.COL1, b.col2 AS TB_col2
FROM   table_A a
       INNER JOIN table_B b
       ON a.col1 = b.col1;

TA_COL1 TA_COL2 TB_COL1 TB_COL2
------- ------- ------- -------
      2 b             2 B
      3 c             3 C
```

Changing to a LEFT JOIN produces the results below. The row in table_A without a matching value in table_B is now displayed. The LEFT JOIN will return rows without matches from the table represented on the left side of the JOIN operator (in this case a.col1).

```
SELECT a.col1 AS TA_COL1, a.col2 AS TA_col2,
       b.col1 AS TB_COL1, b.col2 AS TB_col2
FROM   table_A a
       LEFT JOIN table_B b
       ON a.col1 = b.col1;

TA_COL1 TA_COL2 TB_COL1 TB_COL2
------- ------- ------- -------
      2 b             2 B
      3 c             3 C
      1 a
```

Changing to a RIGHT JOIN produces the results below. Now the row in table_B without a matching value in table_A is now displayed. The RIGHT JOIN will return rows without matches from the table represented on the right side of the JOIN operator (in this case b.col1). We could have gotten the same results by continuing to use the LEFT JOIN but reversing the order of the tables in the FROM clause(i.e. table_B b LEFT JOIN table_A a).

```
SELECT a.col1 AS TA_COL1, a.col2 AS TA_col2,
       b.col1 AS TB_COL1, b.col2 AS TB_col2
FROM   table_A a
       RIGHT JOIN table_B b
       ON a.col1 = b.col1;

TA_COL1 TA_COL2 TB_COL1 TB_COL2
------- ------- ------- -------
      2 b             2 B
      3 c             3 C
                      4 D
```

Changing to a FULL OUTER JOIN produces the results below. In this case, all rows in both tables are returned regardless of whether the condition evaluates to TRUE.

```
SELECT a.col1 AS TA_COL1, a.col2 AS TA_col2,
       b.col1 AS TB_COL1, b.col2 AS TB_col2
FROM   table_A a
       FULL OUTER JOIN table_B b
       ON a.col1 = b.col1;

TA_COL1 TA_COL2 TB_COL1 TB_COL2
------- ------- ------- -------
      2 b             2 B
      3 c             3 C
                      4 D
      1 a
```

# Using Subqueries to Solve Queries

## Define subqueries

Subqueries are generally used to answer questions that contain multiple parts. For example, you might have a need to determine which pilots fly the same type of aircraft as James Thomas. To determine that, it is first necessary to determine which aircraft James pilots. Once the answer to that is located, a second query is required to find out what other pilots fly that same aircraft. This question can be answered by a single select statement that contains an inner query (subquery) that finds James' aircraft and an outer query (parent query) that uses the results of the subquery to filter for pilots with the same aircraft. With the exception of correlated queries, subqueries will always execute before the parent query and the results of the subquery will then be passed to the parent to be used in its execution. There are two classes of subqueries that are determined by their location in the parent query:

- **Inline View**: A subquery in the FROM clause of a SELECT statement. It possible to nest any number of subqueries in an inline view.
- **Nested Subquery**: A subquery in the WHERE clause of a SELECT statement. You can nest up to 255 levels of subqueries in a nested subquery.

The following is an example of an inline query:

```
SELECT apt_name, act_name, sum_seats
FROM   (SELECT apt_name, act_name, SUM(act_seats) sum_seats
        FROM   aircraft_fleet_v
        GROUP BY apt_name, act_name)
ORDER BY sum_seats;
```

```
APT_NAME                  ACT_NAME      SUM_SEATS
------------------------- ------------- ---------
Atlanta, GA               Boeing 737          200
Atlanta, GA               Boeing 757          240
Dallas/Fort Worth         Boeing 767          350
Dallas/Fort Worth         Boeing 747          416
Orlando, FL               Boeing 767          700
Miami, FL                 Boeing 747          832
```

The following is an example of a nested subquery:

```
SELECT emp_first, emp_last, emp_job
FROM   employees emp
WHERE  salary > (SELECT slr_highval
                 FROM   salary_ranges
                 WHERE  slr_code = 'S05');

EMP_FIRST  EMP_LAST   EMP_JOB
---------- ---------- ----------
Big        Boss       CEO
Adam       Smith      CFO
Rick       Jameson    SVP
Rob        Stoner     SVP
Bill       Abong      VP
Janet      Jeckson    VP
```

If columns in a subquery have the same name as columns in the outer query and columns from the outer query are referenced in the subquery, then those columns must be qualified in the subquery. You must prefix all references to the column of the table from the containing statement with the table name or alias. It's good practice to prefix the subquery column references as well, but not a requirement. The following example locates all pilots who have a Boeing 767 as their primary aircraft assignment:

```
SELECT emp_first, emp_last
FROM   employees emp
WHERE  'Boeing 767' = (SELECT act_name
                       FROM   aircraft_fleet_v afl
                       WHERE  afl_id = emp.afl_id);

EMP_FIRST  EMP_LAST
---------- ----------
John       Jones
Top        Gun
Noh        Kia
```

A subquery is a query that is nested inside another SQL statement. The parent might be a SELECT, INSERT, UPDATE, or DELETE statement (or another subquery). Subqueries can return a single row or multiple rows; a single column or multiple columns. A subquery generally executes first and its result then used as part of the outer query. The exception to this is a correlated query which will be discussed later in this section. A subquery can be used in any of the following locations:

- The SELECT list

```
SELECT col1, col2, (SELECT expr FROM table) as sqexp
FROM   table_name;
```

- The FROM clause

```
SELECT col1, col2, col3
FROM  (SELECT col1, col2, col3
       FROM   table_name);
```

- The WHERE clause

```
SELECT col1, col2, col3
FROM   table_name
WHERE col1 = (SELECT col1
              FROM   table_name2);
```

- The HAVING clause

```
SELECT col1, col2, SUM(col3)
FROM   table_name1
GROUP BY col1, col2
HAVING SUM(col3) = (SELECT expr
                    FROM   table_name2);
```

## Describe the types of problems subqueries can solve

There are several ways in which subqueries can be utilized.

### Create a Table Equivalent to SELECT From

A subquery can be used in the FROM clause of a query as a table-equivalent. When used in this fashion, they are called inline views. The subquery is used to format the table data in a fashion that makes it possible for the outer SELECT to return the desired results. Inline views often aggregate data from the base table.

```
SELECT emp_job, avg_sal, min_sal || ' - ' ||  max_sal AS salary_range
FROM   (SELECT emp_job, AVG(salary) AVG_SAL, MIN(salary) MIN_SAL,
MAX(salary) MAX_SAL
        FROM   employees
        GROUP BY emp_job)
ORDER BY max_sal DESC

EMP_JOB    AVG_SAL SALARY_RANGE
---------- ------- -----------------
CEO         197500 197500 - 197500
CFO         157000 157000 - 157000
SVP         147150 145200 - 149100
VP          125650 123500 - 127800
SrDir       111000 110500 - 111500
Mgr         101500 101500 - 101500
Pilot     93156.25 87500 - 98500
```

### Generate a Result Set to Filter by

You might use a subquery to answer questions such as which airports have 747s based at them. You could answer that with a subquery such as the below example.

```
SELECT apt_name, apt_abbr
FROM   airports apt
WHERE  apt.apt_id IN (SELECT apt_id
                      FROM   aircraft_types act
                             INNER JOIN aircraft_fleet afl
                             ON act.act_id = afl.act_id
                      WHERE  act_name = 'Boeing 747')
```

```
APT_NAME                 APT_ABBR
----------------------- --------
Miami, FL                MIA
Dallas/Fort Worth        DFW
```

## Generate Projection Columns

When utilized in the SELECT list of a query, scalar subqueries act like SQL functions to generate new expressions.

```
SELECT emp_first, emp_last, salary,
       (SELECT AVG(salary)
        FROM   employees
        WHERE  emp2.emp_job = emp1.emp_job) AVG_SALARY
FROM   employees
WHERE  emp_job = 'Pilot';

EMP_FIRST  EMP_LAST    SALARY AVG_SALARY
---------- ---------- ------ ----------
John       Jones        97500   88968.75
Top        Gun          91500   88968.75
Phil       McCoy       105000   88968.75
James      Thomas       98500   88968.75
John       Picard       49500   88968.75
Luke       Skytalker    90000   88968.75
Dell       Aptop        87500   88968.75
Noh        Kia          92250   88968.75
```

## Generate Data for an INSERT, UPDATE, or DELETE

A subquery can be used to generate a set of rows to be inserted into a table. Alternately, a scalar subquery could be utilized as the source expression for an update statement. Finally, a subquery could be used to identify rows that meet a given criteria and pass the result to a delete statement.

The following statement would add a new row into the AIRCRAFT_TYPES table for the Boeing 787, pulling some values from the 767. It does not supply a primary key value, so if there were not a trigger in place to provide that data, the INSERT would fail.

```
INSERT INTO aircraft_types (act_name, act_body_style,
            act_decks, act_seats)
SELECT 'Boeing 787', act_body_style, act_decks, 300
FROM   aircraft_types
WHERE  act_name = 'Boeing 767';
```

When using a subquery in an INSERT statement insert data into a table, the VALUES clause is not used. A subquery inside a VALUES clause is illegal and will generate an error. The reverse is also true. An INSERT that is not using a subquery must have the VALUES keyword.

This statement would move all aircraft based in Orlando to Dallas/Ft Worth:

```
UPDATE aircraft_fleet
SET    apt_id = (SELECT apt_id
                 FROM   airports
                 WHERE  apt_abbr = 'DFW')
WHERE  apt_id = (SELECT apt_id
                 FROM   airports
                 WHERE  apt_abbr = 'MCO');
```

The following example would delete any rows from the AIRCRAFT_TYPES table if there is not currently an aircraft of that type in the fleet.

```
DELETE FROM aircraft_types
WHERE  act_id NOT IN (SELECT act_id
                      FROM   aircraft_fleet);
```

## Describe the types of subqueries

At the highest level, there are three classes of subqueries:

**Single-row subqueries**

A single-row subquery returns a single result row to the parent SQL. When only a single column is returned, it is a special subclass called a scalar subquery. Scalar subqueries can be used in almost every location where you can use an expression, literal value, or a constant. The following example uses a scalar subquery to get the average salary for all pilots. The main query then returns all pilots making more than that average.

```
SELECT emp_first, emp_last, salary
FROM   employees emp1
WHERE  emp_job = 'Pilot'
AND    salary > (SELECT AVG(salary)
                 FROM   employees emp2
                 WHERE  emp2.emp_job = emp1.emp_job);

EMP_FIRST  EMP_LAST   SALARY
---------- ---------- ------
John       Jones       97500
Top        Gun         91500
Phil       McCoy      105000
James      Thomas      98500
Luke       Skytalker   90000
Noh        Kia         92250
```

**Multiple-row subqueries** -- A multiple-row subquery returns result sets with more than one row to the surrounding SQL. Often they are used to generate results for a SELECT statement or DML statement. The following statement locates all employees coming up on their tenth-year work anniversary and inserts them into an awards table.

```
INSERT INTO ten_year_awards
(SELECT emp_first, emp_last, emp_job, start_date
 FROM   employees emp1
 WHERE  start_date BETWEEN ADD_MONTHS(sysdate, -140)
                       AND ADD_MONTHS(sysdate, -120)
);
```

**Correlated subqueries** – When a subquery references column data from the parent query, the results become dependent on the parent. Since the parent data can change with each row returned by the parent query, unlike a single or multiple-row subquery that run a single time when a SQL statement is executed, a correlated subquery must run once for each row of the parent. The results can be useful, but correlated subqueries can create performance problems depending on the execute time of the subquery and the number of rows evaluated in the parent query. The following example of a correlated query returns all pilots who are based out of Dallas/Fort Worth.

```
SELECT emp_first, emp_last
FROM   employees emp
WHERE  afl_id IS NOT NULL
AND    'Dallas/Fort Worth' = (SELECT apt_name
                              FROM   aircraft_fleet_v
                              WHERE  afl_id = emp.afl_id);

EMP_FIRST  EMP_LAST
---------- ----------
Dell       Aptop
Noh        Kia
```

## Query data using correlated subqueries

A correlated query occurs when a nested subquery references a column value from table in a parent query one or more levels above the subquery. A correlated subquery is executed once for each row processed by the referenced parent statement. When columns in the subquery comparison have not been qualified, Oracle resolves them by looking first at the subquery and then in the tables in the parent statement. If a column name that exists in both tables is used inside the subquery and is not qualified, Oracle will treat it as belonging to the subquery table. Best practice is to qualify all such column comparisons with the proper table or alias to avoid unintended behavior. Correlated subqueries provide solutions for questions for which the answer depends on a value in each row returned by the parent statement.

```
SELECT emp_first, emp_last, emp_job, salary
FROM   employees emp1
WHERE  salary < (SELECT AVG(salary)
                 FROM   employees emp2
                 WHERE  emp1.emp_job = emp2.emp_job);
```

```
EMP_FIRST  EMP_LAST   EMP_JOB    SALARY
---------- ---------- ---------- ------
Rick       Jameson    SVP        145200
Bill       Abong      VP         123500
Alf        Alien      SrDir      110500
John       Picard     Pilot       49500
Dell       Aptop      Pilot       87500
```

## Update and delete rows using correlated subqueries

Following are examples of using correlated subqueries to DELETE and UPDATE data based on correlated subqueries. The first example deletes any rows from the AIRCRAFT_TYPES table that do not currently exist in the AIRCRAFT_FLEET table.

```
DELETE
FROM   aircraft_types act
WHERE  0 = (SELECT COUNT(*)
            FROM   aircraft_fleet afl
            WHERE  afl.act_id = act.act_id);
```

The second example gives a 5% raise to all of the pilots currently below the average pilot salary .

```
UPDATE employees emp1
SET    salary = TRUNC(salary * 1.05)
WHERE  salary < (SELECT AVG(salary)
                 FROM   employees emp2
                 WHERE  emp1.emp_job = emp2.emp_job)
AND    emp_job = 'Pilot';
```

## Use the EXISTS and NOT EXISTS operators

The EXISTS operator is used to test for the existence of any rows returned by a subquery. When Oracle is testing the condition for an EXISTS operator, the subquery will be executed. If any result row is returned by the subquery, the condition is flagged as TRUE and the execution of the subquery stops. For this reason, EXISTS can be faster than other operations that perform a logically equivalent comparison. For example, you could have a subquery that performs a SELECT COUNT(*) where the outer query looks for a value greater than zero. This would have the same effect as an EXISTS against a subquery performing SELECT * with the same conditions. However, the COUNT(*) operation would have to process every row in the table that met the subquery conditions before returning a result to the parent query. By contrast, an EXISTS condition against a subquery would evaluate to TRUE and stop after hitting a single row that met the specified conditions.

```
SELECT department_id, department_name
FROM   hr.departments dpt
WHERE  EXISTS (SELECT department_id
               FROM   hr.employees emp
               WHERE  dpt.department_id = emp.department_id)

DEPARTMENT_ID DEPARTMENT_NAME
------------- ------------------------------
           10 Administration
           20 Marketing
           30 Purchasing
           40 Human Resources
           50 Shipping
           60 IT
           70 Public Relations
           80 Sales
           90 Executive
          100 Finance
          110 Accounting
```

The NOT EXISTS operator performs the exact opposite evaluation. If any row is returned by the subquery, a FALSE value is returned and the subquery stops processing further rows.

```
SELECT department_id, department_name
FROM   hr.departments dpt
WHERE  NOT EXISTS (SELECT department_id
                   FROM   hr.employees emp
                   WHERE  dpt.department_id = emp.department_id)
```

```
DEPARTMENT_ID DEPARTMENT_NAME
------------- ------------------------------
          120 Treasury
          130 Corporate Tax
          140 Control And Credit
          150 Shareholder Services
          160 Benefits
          170 Manufacturing
          180 Construction
          190 Contracting
          200 Operations
          210 IT Support
          220 NOC
          230 IT Helpdesk
          240 Government Sales
          250 Retail Sales
          260 Recruiting
          270 Payroll
```

## Use the WITH clause

The WITH query_name clause allows you to name a subquery block. Once named, the block can be referenced multiple times in the same query. The database treats the query name as either an inline view or as a temporary table. When treated as a temporary table, the results of running the subquery once are stored in the temporary tablespace and used every time the block is called in the query.

You can specify this clause in any top-level SELECT statement and in most types of subqueries. The query name is visible to the main query and to all subsequent subqueries. For recursive subquery factoring, the query name is even visible to the subquery that defines the query name itself.

In the following example the salaries for each department are calculated in the query named DEPT_COSTS. The results of that query are then averaged in the query named AVG_COST and the result used in the SELECT operation to return only the departments for which the costs are above the average.

```
WITH
  dept_costs AS (
    SELECT department_name, SUM(salary) dept_total
    FROM   hr.employees e
           INNER JOIN hr.departments d
           ON e.department_id = d.department_id
    GROUP BY department_name),
  avg_cost AS (
    SELECT SUM(dept_total)/COUNT(*) avrg
    FROM   dept_costs)
SELECT *
FROM   dept_costs
WHERE  dept_total > (SELECT avrg FROM avg_cost)
ORDER BY department_name;

DEPARTMENT_NAME                DEPT_TOTAL
------------------------------ ----------
Sales                              304500
Shipping                           156400
```

## Use single-row and multiple-row subqueries

Following are some examples of single- and multiple-row subqueries. While either type of subquery may be used in the WHERE and HAVING clauses of the parent query, you must use a valid comparison operator. The two lists below show valid operators for single and multiple row subqueries. It's important to note that while multiple-row operators will work correctly if only a single row is returned by a subquery, the reverse is not true. Single row operators will generate an error if more than one row is returned.

**Single Row Operators**

- **=** -- Equal to
- **>** -- Greater than
- **>=** -- Greater than or equal to
- **<** -- Less than
- **<=** -- Less than or equal to
- **<>** or **!=** -- Not equal to

## Multiple Row Operators

- **IN** -- Equal to any member in a list
- **NOT IN** -- Not equal to any member in a list
- **ANY** -- TRUE when any rows match the comparison value. Must be preceded by <, >, <=, >=, =, or !=.
- **ALL** – TRUE when all rows match the comparison value. Must be preceded by <, >, <=, >=, =, or !=.
- **EXISTS** -- TRUE when the subquery returns any rows
- **NOT EXISTS --** TRUE when the subquery returns no rows

## Single-Row Subquery

The following example has a subquery that pulls the aircraft fleet record for the pilot named Picard. That information is used in the outer query to pull in information about that aircraft.

```
SELECT apt_name, apt_abbr, act_name, act_seats
FROM   airports apt
       INNER JOIN aircraft_fleet afl
       ON apt.apt_id = afl.apt_id
       INNER JOIN aircraft_types act
       ON act.act_id = afl.act_id
WHERE  afl_id = (SELECT afl_id
                 FROM   employees
                 WHERE  emp_last = 'Picard');

APT_NAME               APT_ABBR ACT_NAME     ACT_SEATS
---------------------- -------- ------------ ---------
Miami, FL              MIA      Boeing 747         416
```

## Multiple-Row Subquery

In this example, the only changes are the addition of two more pilots and a change in the operator used for the subquery comparison. The '=' operator has been replaced by the 'IN' operator. The remainder of the query is identical and the result is information about three aircraft instead of one. The previous example could have used the 'IN' operator instead of the '=' operator with no change in functionality.

```
SELECT apt_name, apt_abbr, act_name, act_seats
FROM   airports apt
       INNER JOIN aircraft_fleet afl
       ON apt.apt_id = afl.apt_id
       INNER JOIN aircraft_types act
       ON act.act_id = afl.act_id
WHERE  afl_id IN (SELECT afl_id
                  FROM   employees
                  WHERE  emp_last IN ('Picard', 'McCoy', 'Aptop')
                 );
```

```
APT_NAME               APT_ABBR ACT_NAME     ACT_SEATS
---------------------- -------- ------------ ---------
Atlanta, GA            ATL      Boeing 737         200
Miami, FL              MIA      Boeing 747         416
Dallas/Fort Worth      DFW      Boeing 747         416
```

- Subqueries can include GROUP functions as part of their syntax.
- Subqueries cannot include an ORDER BY clause.
- Subqueries that return no rows evaluate to NULL

# Using the Set Operators

## Describe set operators

Set operators allow you to combine the results from two or more SELECT statements. The results of individual SELECT statements are treated as sets, and SQL set operations are applied against the sets to generate the desired result. Queries joined by set operators are also known as compound queries.

Oracle supports the following set operations:

- **UNION** – Combines the results of two SELECT operations into a single set. Duplicate rows are removed from the end result.
- **UNION ALL** -- Combines the results of two SELECT operations into a single set. Duplicate rows are included in the end result.
- **INTERSECT** – Returns distinct rows where all selected values exist in both queries.
- **MINUS** – Returns distinct rows selected by the first query but not the second.

All set operators have equal precedence. Any time a SQL statement contains multiple set operators, Oracle will evaluate them from top to bottom unless parentheses are used to explicitly specify a different order. The select lists of every query being combined with SET operators must have the same number of columns and each column position must be in the same data type group. For example, column one in the first SELECT could be a VARCHAR2 field and column one in the second SELECT a CHAR field. However, if column one in the first query is a VARCHAR2 field and column one in the second query is a NUMBER field, Oracle will generate an error. It is also possible to use SET operators in subqueries.

Columns names returned by the query are determined by the first SELECT statement. An ORDER BY clause can only be placed at the very end of a compound query involving set operators.

Restrictions on the Set Operators

- Set operations cannot be performed on BLOB, CLOB, BFILE, VARRAY, or nested table columns.
- UNION, INTERSECT, and MINUS operators are not valid on LONG columns.
- Expressions in the SELECT list must have an alias in order to be used in the ORDER BY clause.
- Set operators cannot be used with the for_update_clause.
- Set operations are not allowed on SELECT statements containing TABLE collection expressions.

## Use a set operator to combine multiple queries into a single query

Following are examples of each of the four types of SET operations. For the examples, we'll use the following tables and data:

```
CREATE TABLE table_setA (
  col1      VARCHAR2(1)
);

CREATE TABLE table_setB (
  col1      VARCHAR2(1)
);

INSERT INTO table_setA VALUES ('A');
INSERT INTO table_setA VALUES ('A');
INSERT INTO table_setA VALUES ('A');
INSERT INTO table_setA VALUES ('A');
INSERT INTO table_setA VALUES ('B');
INSERT INTO table_setA VALUES ('C');

INSERT INTO table_setB VALUES ('B');
INSERT INTO table_setB VALUES ('B');
INSERT INTO table_setB VALUES ('C');
INSERT INTO table_setB VALUES ('C');
INSERT INTO table_setB VALUES ('D');
INSERT INTO table_setB VALUES ('D');
INSERT INTO table_setB VALUES ('D');
```

If the UNION set operator is used to combine results from these two tables, it will produce the distinct values returned by the two queries:

```
SELECT col1
FROM   table_setA
UNION
SELECT col1
FROM   table_setB

COL1
----
A
B
C
D
```

If the UNION ALL set operator is used to combine results from these two tables, it will produce all values returned by the two queries. The UNION ALL is the **only** set operator that does not produce distinct results.

```
SELECT col1
FROM   table_setA
UNION ALL
SELECT col1
FROM   table_setB;

COL1
----
A
A
A
A
B
C
B
B
C
C
D
D
D
```

If the INTERSECT set operator is used to combine results from these two tables, it will produce only values returned by both queries.

```
SELECT col1
FROM   table_setA
INTERSECT
SELECT col1
FROM   table_setB;

COL1
----
B
C
```

If the MINUS set operator is used to combine results from these two tables, it will produce only values returned by the first query, but not the second. MINUS is the **only** set operator where the order of the queries will change the results.

```
SELECT col1
FROM   table_setA
MINUS
SELECT col1
FROM   table_setB;

COL1
----
A
```

```
SELECT col1
FROM   table_setB
MINUS
SELECT col1
FROM   table_setA;

COL1
----
D
```

## Control the order of rows returned

By default, the output of compound queries is not sorted. The output of the individual sets will be returned in groups, and the sorting within the groups is largely indeterminate. It is not allowable to make use of ORDER BY clauses in the individual queries. To sort the results of a compound query, you must place an ORDER BY clause at the very end of the SQL statement. This will sort the entire output of the compound query. With compound queries, making use of column position to sort by is often useful because the column names of the components may be different. If you use column names or aliases, you must use those from the topmost SELECT list in the compound query.

The following example performs a SET operation UNIONing rows where the employee has a salary greater than $100,000 with employees who are pilots. Since both rows are coming from the same table, the query could be written more efficiently without a SET operation. This is simply an easy way to generate a SET example. The query contains ORDER BY operations after each of the sets. This is illegal and generates an error:

```
SELECT emp_first, emp_last, emp_job, salary
FROM   employees
WHERE  salary > 100000
ORDER BY emp_last, emp_first
UNION
SELECT emp_first, emp_last, emp_job, salary
FROM   employees
WHERE  emp_job = 'Pilot'
ORDER BY emp_last, emp_first;

SQL Error: ORA-00933: SQL command not properly ended
00933. 00000 -  "SQL command not properly ended"
```

If the first ORDER BY is removed from the query, the data succeeds and orders the rows as expected:

```
SELECT emp_first, emp_last, emp_job, salary
FROM   employees
WHERE  salary > 130000
UNION
SELECT emp_first, emp_last, emp_job, salary
FROM   employees
WHERE  emp_job = 'Pilot'
ORDER BY emp_last, emp_first;
```

```
EMP_FIRST  EMP_LAST   EMP_JOB    SALARY
---------- ---------- ---------- ------
Dell       Aptop      Pilot       87500
Big        Boss       CEO        197500
Top        Gun        Pilot       91500
Rick       Jameson    SVP        145200
John       Jones      Pilot       97500
Noh        Kia        Pilot       92250
Phil       McCoy      Pilot      105000
John       Picard     Pilot       49500
Luke       Skytalker  Pilot       90000
Adam       Smith      CFO        157000
Rob        Stoner     SVP        149100
James      Thomas     Pilot       98500
```

Because the data from multiple sets often have different column names, they are commonly ordered using the column position rather than the column name.

```
SELECT emp_first, emp_last, emp_job, salary
FROM   employees
WHERE  salary > 130000
MINUS
SELECT emp_first, emp_last, emp_job, salary
FROM   employees
WHERE  emp_job = 'Pilot'
ORDER BY 2, 1;
```

```
EMP_FIRST  EMP_LAST   EMP_JOB    SALARY
---------- ---------- ---------- ------
Big        Boss       CEO        197500
Rick       Jameson    SVP        145200
Adam       Smith      CFO        157000
Rob        Stoner     SVP        149100
```

# Manipulating Data

## Truncate data

While the Oracle TRUNCATE command is included under a section called 'Manipulating Data', it should be noted that this is **not** a DML command like everything else in this section but rather a DDL command. The TRUNCATE command performs a function similar to the DELETE command, but there are significant differences in how that action is performed.

When deleting a large number of rows, it is possible, even likely, that the operation may take quite some time to complete. There can be a great deal of overhead to DELETE operations. A significant portion of DELETE overhead comes from the need to store the UNDO information for each row so that the operation can be rolled back. When you delete every row in a table, all of the data in that table gets written out to UNDO simultaneously with being removed from the original table. There may also be DELETE triggers that fire for each row. There may be index records for each row to get removed. The time to perform these operations adds up and make large deletes an expensive operation.

The TRUNCATE is often portrayed as 'a fast DELETE'. That is not really accurate. The result of a TRUNCATE operation is in several ways closer to dropping the table and recreating it. When a DELETE is performed on a table, whether it is one row or a million rows, Oracle removes the rows one at a time iteratively until all of the rows covered by the DELETE statement are gone. The TRUNCATE operation effectively performs a single data dictionary operation that marks the table as empty. No WHERE clause can be applied to it and no UNDO information is stored because the data is not really being manipulated. TRUNCATE is a DDL operation and performs its work in the data dictionary. It cannot be reversed if it was performed in error by either a ROLLBACK or a FLASHBACK TABLE operation. The syntax of a TRUNCATE is:

```
TRUNCATE TABLE table_name;
```

TRUNCATE is much faster and more efficient of database resources than a DELETE statement. It generates much less overhead and completes within a second or two. By default, Oracle will also perform the following tasks during a TRUNCATE operation:

- Deallocate all space used by the removed rows except that specified by MINEXTENTS.
- Set the NEXT storage parameter to the size of the last extent removed from the segment by the TRUNCATE operation.

There are several restrictions to TRUNCATE operations:

- If a table contains the parent key of a foreign key constraint, it is not possible to TRUNCATE the table while the constraint is enabled.
- When a temporary table is TRUNCATEd, only the rows created during the current session are removed.
- A table that is part of a cluster cannot be individually truncated.
- If a domain index is defined on table, then neither the index nor any index partitions can be marked IN_PROGRESS.
- You cannot truncate the parent table of a reference-partitioned table.

## Insert rows into a table

Data Manipulation Language (DML) is the name given to the SQL statements used to manage data in the Oracle database. DML statements include INSERT, UPDATE, DELETE and MERGE. The SELECT statement could technically be considered a DML statement but is seldom considered one in practice. As a general rule, only commands which add, alter, or remove rows from database tables are considered to be data manipulation statements. However, if SELECT is not included with DML, then it has no place to be. It is certainly not Data Definition Language

(DDL) or Data Control Language (DCL). Just be aware that when reference is made to DML statements, the context probably does not include SELECT operations.

Data manipulation language statements are utilized to manage data in existing schema objects. DML statements do not modify information in the data dictionary and do not implicitly commit the current transaction. The most commonly identified DML commands are:

- **INSERT** – Used to populate data in tables. It is possible to insert one row into one table, one row into multiple tables, multiple rows into one table, or multiple rows into multiple tables.
- **UPDATE** – Used to alter data that has already been inserted into a database table. An UPDATE can affect a single row or multiple rows, and a single column or multiple columns. The WHERE clause will determine which rows in the table are altered. When executed with no WHERE clause, it will update all rows in the target table. A single UPDATE statement can only act on one table.
- **DELETE** – Used to remove previously inserted rows from a table. The command can remove a single row or multiple rows from a table. When executed with no WHERE clause, it will remove all rows from the target table. It is not possible to delete individual columns – the entire row is deleted or it is not.
- **MERGE** – Used for hybrid DML operations. The MERGE can insert, update and delete rows in a table all in a single statement. There is no operation that a MERGE can perform that could not be performed by a combination of INSERT, UPDATE and DELETE.

You can add new rows to an Oracle table with the INSERT statement. The syntax of a single table INSERT is:

```
INSERT INTO table_name [(column [,column…])]
VALUES (value [, value…]);
```

In this statement, table_name is the table into which rows will be inserted, column is the name of the column(s) of the table values are being added to, and value is the data that will be inserted into the column. The column list is optional, but if omitted, the values clause must include all columns of the table in the order that they are recorded in the Oracle data dictionary. A column list allows you to insert into a subset of the table columns and explicitly match the order of the columns to the order of the values list. When writing SQL that will be reused (such as in a stored PL/SQL procedure) is best practice to always explicitly list the columns in an insert statement. This makes the resulting code more robust if columns are added to the table at a later date. When there are multiple rows or columns, they are enclosed by parentheses and separated by commas.

The simplest form of an insert statement inserts a single row into a single table. The following inserts a new person into the EMPLOYEES table (described below).

```
desc employees
Name           Null     Type
-------------- -------- ------------
EMP_ID         NOT NULL NUMBER
AFL_ID                  NUMBER
EMP_FIRST               VARCHAR2(10)
EMP_LAST       NOT NULL VARCHAR2(10)
EMP_JOB                 VARCHAR2(10)
EMP_SUPERVISOR          NUMBER
SALARY                  NUMBER
START_DATE              DATE


INSERT INTO employees (emp_id, afl_id, emp_first,
                       emp_last, emp_job,
                       emp_supervisor, salary,
                       start_date)
VALUES (18, NULL, 'Guy', 'Newberry', 'Mgr', 8,
        98250, '07-JAN-2012');
```

Note that character data is enclosed by quotes as is the one date field. Numeric values being inserted into a NUMBER column are not generally enclosed by quotes, but it will not generate an error if you do (Oracle will implicitly convert the value back to a number data type during the INSERT operation). The NULL keyword cannot be enclosed in quotes. If the text

NULL was enclosed in quotes, instead of a NULL value being inserted, the text 'NULL' would be inserted (or an error generated if the column were not a character field)..

The above INSERT statement contains all of the values of the EMPLOYEES table and the column order matches that in the data dictionary. The column list is therefore optional and the INSERT could have been written like this:

```
INSERT INTO employees
VALUES (18, NULL, 'Guy', 'Newberry', 'Mgr', 8,
        98250, '07-JAN-2012');
```

To insert into only a subset of columns in a table, you must provide a list of the columns that you wish to provide values for. Any columns not provided in the column list will contain a NULL after the INSERT operation unless they have a default value or are populated by a trigger. The following statement would insert a row into the employees table, leaving the SALARY and START_DATE fields NULL. Note that if either of the columns had a NOT NULL constraint, then the statement would fail.

```
INSERT INTO employees (emp_id, afl_id, emp_first, emp_last,
                       emp_job, emp_supervisor)
VALUES (18, NULL, 'Guy', 'Newberry', 'Mgr', 8);
```

The same operation could have been performed without a column list by explicitly adding the NULL values to the INSERT statement:

```
INSERT INTO employees
VALUES (18, NULL, 'Guy', 'Newberry', 'Mgr', 8, NULL, NULL);
```

**DEFAULT column values**

If a column in the table that is being inserted into contains a DEFAULT value, you can make use of that value by using DEFAULT in your VALUES clause. In the example below, a DEFAULT is added to the start_date field such that is will use the current system date. An insert is then performed explicitly using DEFAULT as the value for the START_DATE column:

```
ALTER TABLE employees MODIFY(start_date DEFAULT SYSDATE);
table EMPLOYEES altered.

INSERT INTO employees (emp_id, afl_id, emp_first, emp_last,
                       emp_job, emp_supervisor, salary,
                       start_date)
VALUES (18, NULL, 'Guy', 'Newberry', 'Mgr', 8, 90000, DEFAULT);
1 rows inserted.

SELECT emp_first, emp_last,  start_date
FROM   employees
WHERE  emp_last='Newberry';

EMP_FIRST  EMP_LAST   START_DATE
---------- ---------- ----------
Guy        Newberry   11-APR-12
```

Instead of using the DEFAULT keyword, the INSERT could have simply ignored the START_DATE column such as the below example:

```
INSERT INTO employees (emp_id, afl_id, emp_first, emp_last,
                       emp_job, emp_supervisor, salary)
VALUES (18, NULL, 'Guy', 'Newberry', 'Mgr', 8, 90000);
1 rows inserted.

SELECT emp_first, emp_last,  start_date
FROM   employees
WHERE  emp_last='Newberry';

EMP_FIRST  EMP_LAST   START_DATE
---------- ---------- ----------
Guy        Newberry   11-APR-12
```

However, if the field is included in the INSERT and VALUES clauses and a NULL is explicitly inserted, then this will override the DEFAULT value of the column (unless the new 12c 'ON NULL' clause has been used with the default):

```
INSERT INTO employees (emp_id, afl_id, emp_first, emp_last,
                       emp_job, emp_supervisor, salary,
                       start_date)
VALUES (18, NULL, 'Guy', 'Newberry', 'Mgr', 8, 90000, NULL);
```

```
1 rows inserted.

SELECT emp_first, emp_last,  start_date
FROM   employees
WHERE  emp_last='Newberry';

EMP_FIRST  EMP_LAST   START_DATE
---------- ---------- ----------
Guy        Newberry
```

You might assume that the START_DATE column could be omitted from the INSERT without an explicit column list and that Oracle would automatically fill the field with the current date. However, you would be wrong in making that assumption:

```
INSERT INTO employees
VALUES (19, NULL, 'Test', 'Osterone', 'Mgr', 8, 92350);

SQL Error: ORA-00947: not enough values
00947. 00000 -  "not enough values"
```

When a column list is not explicitly provided, the SQL parser expects to find values for every column in the table. When a column list is provided and does not contain all columns in the table, Oracle will automatically attempt to fill the remaining columns. If the column has a default value, it will be used. If the column does not have a default value, then Oracle will attempt to fill it with a NULL. As noted earlier, that attempt will fail if the column has a NOT NULL constraint.

### Insert using subquery

In lieu of providing values explicitly for an INSERT statement, it's possible to generate data through a SELECT statement. The following operation inserts a row into the AIRCRAFT_TYPES table using a subquery against the same table. A subquery used for such an operation can be against any table that will produce the data required. When inserting using a subquery, the VALUES keyword is not used. The number and order of columns returned by the subquery must match the number and order of columns in the INSERT statement. The same rules mentioned above apply to inserted data generated through a SELECT operation. The columns of the table being inserted into can be named explicitly or not. If not named, the SELECT must return the same count of columns as the target table.

```
INSERT INTO aircraft_types (act_name, act_body_style,
                            act_decks, act_seats)
SELECT 'Boeing 787', act_body_style, act_decks, 300
FROM   aircraft_types;
```

## Update rows in a table

An UPDATE operation is used to modify existing data in a table. You can update a single row in a table, multiple rows using a filter, or the entire table. If an update does not contain a WHERE clause, every single row in the target table will be updated. The syntax for an UPDATE is:

```
UPDATE table_name
SET    column1 = value1 [, column2 = value2, …]
[WHERE condition];
```

The following statement moves all of the employees that used to report to the employees with emp_id 9 to the new employee with emp_id 18. If no WHERE clause were supplied, all rows in the employees table would have the emp_supervisor field  set to 18.

```
UPDATE employees
SET    emp_supervisor = 18
WHERE  emp_supervisor = 9;
```

The EMP_LAST column of the EMPLOYEES table has a NOT NULL constraint. Trying to set this field to NULL will generate an error:

```
UPDATE employees
SET    emp_last = NULL
WHERE  emp_id = 12;
```

```
SQL Error: ORA-01407: cannot update
("OCPGURU"."EMPLOYEES"."EMP_LAST") to NULL
01407. 00000 -  "cannot update (%s) to NULL"
```

As with the INSERT statement, it's possible to use a subquery to provide the data used for an UPDATE operation. The column count and order must match between the UPDATE and the results generated by the subquery. The syntax for this is:

```
UPDATE table_name
SET    (column1 [, column2 ...] = (SELECT column1 [, column2 ...] FROM
sqtab)
[WHERE condition];
```

## Delete rows from a table

The DELETE operation removes rows that already exist in a table. The syntax for a DELETE statement is:

```
DELETE
[FROM]  table_name
[WHERE  condition];
```

Only the keyword DELETE and a table name are required. If you issue the command 'DELETE employees', then all rows in the EMPLOYEES table will be deleted. The FROM keyword is seldom left off of DELETE statements in practice, but it is strictly optional. The following statement deletes from the EMPLOYEES table the employee with emp_id 9.

```
DELETE
FROM   employees
WHERE  emp_id = 9;
```

There is no data to be supplied for a DELETE operation as there is with INSERT and UPDATE operations. However, it's possible to use a subquery in the WHERE clause to dynamically build the filter of rows to be deleted.

The following query would remove any aircraft from the AIRCRAFT_TYPES table that did not currently exist in the fleet.

```
DELETE FROM aircraft_types
WHERE  act_name NOT IN
       (SELECT act_name
        FROM   aircraft_fleet_v);
```

## Control transactions

A transaction is composed of one or more DML statements punctuated by either a COMMIT or a ROLLBACK command. Transactions are a major part of the mechanism for ensuring the database maintains data integrity. The transaction control statements available in Oracle follow. Only the first three of the below TCL statements are likely to appear on the exam. The last two are for more advanced SQL operations.

- **COMMIT** – Used to end the current transaction and make permanent all changes performed in it.
- **ROLLBACK** -- Used to undo work done in the current transaction or to manually undo the work done by an in-doubt distributed transaction.
- **SAVEPOINT** -- Used to create a name for a specific system change number (SCN), which can be rolled back to at a later date.
- **SET TRANSACTION** – Used to establish the current transaction as read-only or read/write, establish its isolation level, assign it to a specified rollback segment, or assign a name to it.
- **SET CONSTRAINT** -- Used to specify, for a particular transaction, whether a deferrable constraint is checked following each DML statement (IMMEDIATE) or when the transaction is committed (DEFERRED).

A transaction begins when an initial DML statement is issued against the database. This can be followed by any number of additional DML statements. The transaction will continue until one of the following events occurs:

- A COMMIT or ROLLBACK statement is issued
- A DDL statement is issued (DDL statements issue an implicit COMMIT)
- The user exits SQL*Plus or SQL Developer
- SQL*Plus or SQL Developer terminates abnormally.
- The database shuts down abnormally (a crash or shutdown abort).

When performing DML operations, if transaction control is left to only the COMMIT and ROLLBACK commands, the only options to complete a transaction are to accept everything that has been changed and make the changes permanent or accept nothing and undo everything since the last COMMIT. The SAVEPOINT transaction control statement of Oracle allows there to be a middle ground between the two. With save points, you can identify specific locations within the transaction that you can go back to – undoing any DML statements later than that point, but leaving intact all the ones prior to it. The example below shows an example of save points.

```
COMMIT;
INSERT INTO employees (emp_id, afl_id, emp_first, emp_last,
                       emp_job, emp_supervisor)
VALUES (30, NULL, 'Adam', 'Apple', 'Pilot', 9);

INSERT INTO employees (emp_id, afl_id, emp_first, emp_last,
                       emp_job, emp_supervisor)
VALUES (31, NULL, 'Bob', 'Hopeful', 'Pilot', 9);

SAVEPOINT A;

INSERT INTO employees (emp_id, afl_id, emp_first, emp_last,
                       emp_job, emp_supervisor)
VALUES (32, NULL, 'Charlie', 'Chafing', 'Pilot', 9);

INSERT INTO employees (emp_id, afl_id, emp_first, emp_last,
                       emp_job, emp_supervisor)
VALUES (33, NULL, 'Dude', 'Whersmicar', 'Pilot', 9);

SAVEPOINT B;

INSERT INTO employees (emp_id, afl_id, emp_first, emp_last,
                       emp_job, emp_supervisor)
VALUES (33, NULL, 'Ed', 'Horse', 'Pilot', 9);
```

There are three places that this transaction can be rolled back to.

- **ROLLBACK TO SAVEPOINT B** – Will undo only the last INSERT statement.
- **ROLLBACK TO SAVEPOINT A** – Will undo the last three INSERT statements.
- **ROLLBACK** – Will undo all five INSERT statements.

Note that any DDL operations will end a transaction immediately with an implicit commit. Any SAVEPOINT prior to that operation can no longer be rolled back to. Also, if within the same transaction you reuse a save point name, then any ROLLBACK to that save point will only undo to the latest one of that name – the earlier one of that name is deleted automatically when the newer one is created..

**Uncommited Transactions**

Uncommitted transactions in Oracle are in limbo – it's not certain whether they will ever be permanent and so there is limited access to them. Until the point that the transactions have been committed, it is possible to back out the changes with a ROLLBACK. Because they might be reversed, the data required to do so must be retained in the undo segment indefinitely until the changes are either committed or rolled back. Pending transactions have the following four characteristics:

- The changed data is visible to the user that issued the DML.
- The changed data is NOT visible to any other user.
- The rows with the changed data are locked and cannot be altered by any user other than the one with the ongoing transaction.
- The data that existed prior to the DML operation can be recovered by rolling back the transaction.

**Committed Transactions**

Committed transactions in Oracle have been made permanent (although obviously they can be changed with another DML operation). Since they have been made permanent, the portion of the undo segment holding the prior data is released for reuse, and the changed rows are made accessible. Committed transactions have the following four characteristics:

- The changed data is visible to all database users.
- The locks on the rows affected by the DML are released and they can be updated by any user with the correct privileges.
- The changed data has been made permanent and cannot be reversed with a ROLLBACK.
- Any SAVEPOINTs from the transaction are deleted.

If a DML statement fails due to an error, a constraint violation or some other cause, Oracle will roll the statement back. If there are earlier uncommitted DML operations that succeeded without error, they will not be affected by the rollback of the failed statement. If the failed statement is itself a reason for reversing the earlier DML statements, you can issue an explicit rollback. If the statement can be repaired, then you can fix the failed statement and continue on with the remaining portion of the transaction without having to re-issue the preceding DML operations.

# Using DDL Statements to Create and Manage Tables

## Describe data types that are available for columns

Every value contained within the Oracle Database has a data type. The data type associates a given set of properties with the value and causes Oracle to treat the values differently. For example, it is possible to add, subtract, or multiply two values of the NUMBER data type, but not two values of a LONG data type. Any time a table is created, each of its columns must have a data type specified. Data types define the domain of values that each column can contain. There are a number of built-in data types in Oracle and it is possible to create user-defined types that can be used as data types. The data types available for columns are:

- **VARCHAR2(n)** -- Variable-length character string of n characters or bytes.
- **NVARCHAR2(n)** -- Variable-length Unicode character string of n characters.
- **NUMBER** -- Number having optional precision and scale values.
- **FLOAT** -- A subtype of the NUMBER data type having precision but no scale.
- **LONG** -- Character data of variable length up to 2 gigabytes.
- **DATE** -- This data type contains the datetime fields YEAR, MONTH, DAY, HOUR, MINUTE, and SECOND. It does not have fractional seconds or a time zone.
- **BINARY_FLOAT** -- 32-bit floating point number.
- **BINARY_DOUBLE** -- 64-bit floating point number.
- **TIMESTAMP** -- This data type contains the datetime fields YEAR, MONTH, DAY, HOUR, MINUTE, and SECOND. It contains fractional seconds but does not have a time zone.
- **TIMESTAMP WITH TIME ZONE** -- This data type contains the datetime fields YEAR, MONTH, DAY, HOUR, MINUTE, SECOND, TIMEZONE_HOUR, and TIMEZONE_MINUTE. It has fractional seconds and an explicit time zone.
- **TIMESTAMP WITH LOCAL TIME ZONE** – Identical to TIMESTAMP WITH TIME ZONE, with the exceptions that data is normalized to the database time zone when it is stored in the database, and displayed in the current session time zone when retrieved.

- **INTERVAL DAY TO SECOND** -- Stores a period of time in days, hours, minutes, and seconds
- **RAW(n)** -- Raw binary data of length n bytes.
- **LONG RAW** -- Raw binary data of variable length up to 2 gigabytes.
- **ROWID** -- Base 64 string representing the unique address of a row in its table.
- **UROWID** -- Base 64 string representing the logical address of a row of an index-organized table.
- **CHAR(n)** -- Fixed-length character data of length n bytes or characters.
- **NCHAR(n)** -- Fixed-length character data of length n characters.
- **CLOB** -- A character large object containing single-byte or multibyte characters.
- **NCLOB** -- A character large object containing Unicode characters.
- **BLOB** -- A binary large object.
- **BFILE** -- Contains a locator to a large binary file stored outside the database.

## Create a simple table

At its most basic, an Oracle create table statement would look something like the following:

```
CREATE TABLE ocp_example (
  ocp_id                    NUMBER,
  ocp_name                  VARCHAR2(20),
  ocp_date                  DATE);
```

The statement can be broken down into the reserved words CREATE and TABLE, followed by a name for the table, and the column list. The column list must be enclosed in parentheses, and contain column name/data type pairs separated by commas. The table name and the column names must follow Oracle naming rules (discussed next). The SQL statement will be terminated by a semicolon.

A slightly more complex CREATE TABLE statement is below. In addition to defining the column data types, it adds a NOT NULL constraint to the EMP_LAST column and sets the EMP_ID column as the primary key of the table. In addition, it creates a default for the START_DATE column of SYSDATE.

```
CREATE TABLE employees (
  emp_id                  NUMBER,
  afl_id                  NUMBER,
  emp_first               VARCHAR2(10),
  emp_last                VARCHAR2(10) NOT NULL,
  emp_job                 VARCHAR2(10),
  emp_supervisor          NUMBER,
  salary                  NUMBER,
  start_date              DATE DEFAULT SYSDATE,
    PRIMARY KEY (EMP_ID)
);
```

Another way to create a table is by using a CREATE TABLE AS SELECT (CTAS) operation. CTAS statements make use of an existing table to form the basis for the structure (and possibly the contents) of a new table. A CTAS statement can copy all, or only some of the existing columns of an existing table, and likewise all or only a portion of the data. The following statement would create a table called EMPLOYEES_COPY that contained the emp_first, emp_last, emp_job, and start_date columns of EMPLOYEES, and all employees hired in the past year. Tables created via CTAS statement will inherit NOT NULL constraints from the parent table, but no others.

```
CREATE TABLE employees_copy
AS SELECT emp_first, emp_last, emp_job, start_date
   FROM   employees
   WHERE  start_date > SYSDATE - 365;
```

**Database Object Naming Rules**

Every object in the database must have a name. The names may be represented with either a quoted identifier or a nonquoted identifier. A quoted identifier is enclosed in double quotation marks ("). A nonquoted identifier uses no punctuation. Quoted identifiers allow many of the Oracle database naming rules to be circumvented. However, Oracle does not recommend doing so. A complete list of the naming conventions is available in the Oracle SQL reference. A partial list follows:

- Names must be 1 to 30 bytes long with the exception of database names (8 bytes) and database links (128 bytes).
- Nonquoted identifiers cannot be Oracle SQL reserved words.
- Nonquoted identifiers must begin with an alphabetic character.
- Nonquoted identifiers can contain only alphanumeric characters from your database character set and the underscore (_), dollar sign ($), and pound sign (#).
- Nonquoted identifiers are not case sensitive. Oracle interprets them as uppercase. Quoted identifiers are case sensitive.
- Columns in the same table or view cannot have the same name. However, columns in different tables or views can have the same name.
- Within a namespace, no two objects can have the same name.

**Namespaces**

Namespaces are a construct that Oracle uses when locating a database object during the execution of a SQL command. In any single namespace, you may not have more than one object of the same. Each schema in the database has its own namespaces for the objects it contains.

The following schema objects share one namespace:

- Tables
- Views
- Sequences
- Private synonyms
- Stand-alone procedures
- Stand-alone stored functions
- Packages
- Materialized views

- User-defined types

The following schema objects each has its own namespace:

- Indexes
- Constraints
- Clusters
- Database triggers
- Private database links
- Dimensions

The upshot of this is that because tables and views are in the same namespace, you may not have a table and a view with the exact same name for a given schema. Likewise a table and a private synonym of the same name aren't allowed or a sequence and a view. However, indexes are in a separate namespace, so you could have a table and an index of the same name. In addition, because each schema has its own namespace, you could have tables of the same name in multiple schemas.

### Schema References

When performing DML operations against objects that exist in the current schema, the object name is sufficient for Oracle to locate it and execute the operation against it. However, when an object exists in another schema, the object name must be prefixed by the schema name. For example, the departments table exists in the HR schema on the system used in creating this guide. Selecting from this table without a schema reference generates an error:

```
SELECT *
FROM   departments
WHERE  department_id < 70;

ORA-00942: table or view does not exist
00942. 00000 -  "table or view does not exist"
```

If the table name is prefixed by the schema name and a period, the SELECT operation succeeds:

```
SELECT *
FROM   hr.departments
WHERE  department_id < 70;

DEPARTMENT_ID DEPARTMENT_NAME   MANAGER_ID LOCATION_ID
------------- ----------------- ---------- -----------
           10 Administration    200        1700
           20 Marketing         201        1800
           30 Purchasing        114        1700
           40 Human Resources   203        2400
           50 Shipping          121        1500
           60 IT                103        1400
```

## Altering a Table

Once a table has been created, any changes to its structure must be applied using the ALTER TABLE statement. Many of the options available during table creation can also be performed after it exists. The ALTER TABLE statement can be used to perform the following actions (among others – see the Oracle SQL Reference Guide for a complete list):

- Adding new columns
- Modifying existing column definitions
- Dropping existing columns
- Setting existing columns to UNUSED
- Renaming columns
- Adding or removing column constraints
- Adding default values to columns

## Dropping a Table

If there is no longer a need for a table, you can use the DROP TABLE command to remove it from the data dictionary. By default, when a table is dropped in Oracle, it is not removed completely, but placed into a recycle bin. While the table is in the bin, it is possible to restore it. If you drop the table using the optional PURGE keyword, the table and its data will be dropped completely – bypassing the recycle bin. Until the table is purged from the recycle bin, no space is freed in the tablespace datafile from the table drop. In addition, the space used by the dropped table still counts against the QUOTA for the owning user.

When a table is dropped, the action has varying effects on objects related to it. Some database objects that have a dependency on the table, such as views and stored PL/SQL, are invalidated. Other types of dependent objects, such as indexes, triggers, constraints, and object privileges for the table are dropped when the table is. These have no reason to exist when the table is gone. Any synonyms that point to the table are unaffected by the DROP operation as they have no dependencies. Any sequences referenced by table triggers are likewise unaffected (the table is dependent on the sequence via the trigger, not the other way around)

## Create constraints for tables

Constraints are database objects that are used to restrict (constrain) the data allowed into table columns. They are essentially rules that must be met in order for a value to be acceptable. There are several different kinds of constraints available in Oracle:

- **PRIMARY KEY** – The primary key of a table defines a column, or set of columns that must be unique for every row of a table. To satisfy a primary key constraint, none of the column(s) making up the key may be NULL, and the combination of values in the column(s) must be unique. A table can have only a single primary key constraint defined (all other constraint types can exist multiple times in the same table).
- **UNIQUE** – A unique key defines a column or set of columns that must be unique for every row of a table. Unlike a primary key constraint, the UNIQUE constraint does not prevent NULL values in the columns(s) comprising the constraint.

- **NOT NULL** – A NOT NULL constraint prevents a table column from having NULL values. If a column with a UNIQUE constraint is also defined as NOT NULL, it will have the same restrictive behavior as a PRIMARY KEY.
- **FOREIGN KEY** – Foreign keys are also referred to as Referential Integrity constraints. A foreign key constraint ties a column value in one table to a primary or unique key value in another. Values may not be inserted in the table with the reference constraint that do not exist in the referenced key.
- **CHECK** – Check constraints allow for custom conditions to be specified for a column. The conditions must evaluate to TRUE for the operation altering the column value to succeed.

Constraints in Oracle are created by one of two methods. They can be created simultaneously with the table during the CREATE TABLE statement. Alternately they can be created on a table that already exists using the ALTER TABLE statement. There is no such thing as a 'CREATE CONSTRAINT' command. The SQL statement below creates a table with two constraints:

```
CREATE TABLE aircraft_types (
  act_id              NUMBER,
  act_name            VARCHAR2(20),
  act_body_style      VARCHAR2(10),
  act_decks           NUMBER,
  act_seats           NUMBER  NOT NULL
    CONSTRAINT ac_type_pk PRIMARY KEY (act_id)
);
```

Beyond creating the table and columns with associated data types, it contains the instructions for adding two constraints.

- The **act_seats** column has been assigned a NOT NULL constraint. If an insert to this table doesn't reference this column, or references it but attempts to add a NULL value to the column, an error will occur. Because no name was specified for the constraint, Oracle will give it a system-generated name. This is an in-line constraint definition because it is added in the same line as the column. NULL and NOT NULL constraints **must** be defined in-line during a CREATE or ALTER TABLE statements.

- The **act_id** column has been assigned a primary key constraint, and the constraint given the name 'ac_type_pk'. Oracle will create an index of the same name to enforce the primary key constraint. This constraint has been defined out-of-line.

In the example above, the PRIMARY KEY constraint definition was listed at the end of the statement rather than with the column. This is known as out-of-line constraint definition. The following is equivalent to the first SQL statement, with the primary key constraint being defined inline. The end result of a constraint defined inline or out-of-line is identical.

```
CREATE TABLE aircraft_types (
  act_id              NUMBER   CONSTRAINT ac_type_pk
                               PRIMARY KEY,
  act_name            VARCHAR2(20),
  act_body_style      VARCHAR2(10),
  act_decks           NUMBER,
  act_seats           NUMBER   NOT NULL
);
```

It's possible to view these constraints by querying the USER_CONSTRAINTS view for all constraints associated with the AIRCRAFT_TYPES table. Note that the AC_TYPE_PK constraint is type P (Primary Key), and has no search condition. It is enforced by an index, not by a condition. By contrast the NOT NULL constraint is type 'C' which stands for 'Check.' A NOT NULL constraint is a specific type of check constraint, and always has a condition that indicates the column should be NOT NULL.

```
SELECT constraint_name, constraint_type, search_condition
FROM   user_constraints
WHERE  table_name = 'AIRCRAFT_TYPES'

CONSTRAINT_NAME CONSTRAINT_TYPE SEARCH_CONDITION
--------------- --------------- -----------------------
AC_TYPE_PK      P
SYS_C007066     C               "ACT_SEATS" IS NOT NULL
```

## Drop columns and set column UNUSED

The DROP option of the ALTER TABLE statement allows you to permanently remove one or more columns from a table. If a column is not being utilized, dropping it will free up space and potentially improve performance. There are two variants of the drop column syntax:

```
ALTER TABLE constraint_test
DROP COLUMN col2;

ALTER TABLE constraint_test
DROP (col2);
```

The first variant allows you to drop a single column from a table. The second variant has the capability to drop multiple columns at once. To drop more than one column, you would list them all in the parentheses, separated by commas. It is possible to drop all but one column of the table (a table cannot exist with zero columns).

If dropping a column that is referenced by a foreign key constraint, you would need to add the CASCADE CONSTRAINTS clause to the statement. This would cause any associated foreign key constraints to be dropped at the same time as the column.

```
ALTER TABLE constraint_test
DROP COLUMN col2 CASCADE CONSTRAINTS;
```

There is a second approach to removing a column from a table. You may use the SET UNUSED clause of the ALTER TABLE statement to make a column **permanently** unusable. SET UNUSED is simply a precursor to dropping the column – it's not a halfway measure that you can change back at some point in the future. In all ways except for recovering the space used by the column, SET UNUSED is equivalent to DROP COLUMN in its behavior. The only reason to set a column unused rather than dropping is if it is important that the column be made inaccessible immediately, but it's not feasible to take the performance hit required when dropping a column. For example, dropping a column of a multi-million row table would cause a good bit of disk and database activity as the entire table is updated. The SET UNUSED command, by contrast, simply updates the data dictionary and so is instant and low impact. Just as with the DROP option, there are two variants of SET UNUSED that allow you to set one column unused or multiple columns

```
ALTER TABLE constraint_test
SET UNUSED COLUMN col2;

ALTER TABLE constraint_test
SET UNUSED (col2);
```

At some future point, presumably at a time of low usage, the column will be dropped using the DROP UNUSED COLUMNS clause. Until the unused column(s) have been dropped, the column data continues to be physically present in the table (albeit completely inaccessible). The command to drop columns in a table that have been marked unused is:

```
ALTER TABLE constraint_test
DROP UNUSED COLUMNS;
```

## Create and use external tables

The external tables feature in Oracle allows you to access data in external files as if it were in a table in the database. To create an external table, you must know the file format and record format of the data source that will be used for the table. External tables are created using the ORGANIZATION EXTERNAL option of the CREATE TABLE statement. When creating an external table, you specify the following attributes:

- **TYPE** -- The two external table types are ORACLE_LOADER, and ORACLE_DATAPUMP. The ORACLE_LOADER access driver is the default. It can not write to the file, only read, and the data must come from a text file. The ORACLE_DATAPUMP access driver can read from and write to external binary dump files.

- **DEFAULT DIRECTORY** -- Specifies the default location of the external files. The location must be specified using an Oracle directory object. The directory object must exist prior to the creation of the EXTERNAL TABLE.
- **ACCESS PARAMETERS** -- Specify the information about the external data source required for the access driver to be able to read it. The two access types have distinct parameter requirements. The access parameters are also referred to as the opaque_format_spec in the CREATE TABLE...ORGANIZATION EXTERNAL statement.
- **LOCATION** -- Indicates the location of the external data. The file locations are paired directory objects and filenames. If no directory is specified, then the default directory object is used.

The following example shows the use of each of these attributes:

```
CREATE TABLE emp_load
  (emp_number       CHAR(5),
   emp_dob          CHAR(20),
   emp_last_name    CHAR(20),
   emp_first_name   CHAR(15),
   emp_middle_name  CHAR(15),
   emp_hire_date    DATE)
ORGANIZATION EXTERNAL
  (TYPE ORACLE_LOADER
   DEFAULT DIRECTORY def_dir1
   ACCESS PARAMETERS
     (RECORDS DELIMITED BY NEWLINE
      FIELDS (emp_number       CHAR(2),
              emp_dob          CHAR(20),
              emp_last_name    CHAR(18),
              emp_first_name   CHAR(11),
              emp_middle_name  CHAR(11),
              emp_hire_date    CHAR(10)
                   date_format DATE mask "mm/dd/yyyy"
             )
     )
   LOCATION ('info.dat')
  );
```

Once created, external tables act in most ways like an internal table. There is no special syntax when querying them via a SELECT statement. It's not possible to create indexes on them and every query against them effectively performs a full-table scan, so performance can be an issue with large files. Even when performing a specific query against what would normally be considered a 'primary key' field, Oracle must scan every single row in the file before the query is complete. Because the files making up an external table are not really part of the database, transferring them between databases is easy.

# Managing Objects with Data Dictionary Views

## Query various data dictionary views

The data dictionary of Oracle contains every single piece of information about the tables, indexes, views, synonyms, procedures, and every other type of object that exists in the database. If you know where to look (and have sufficient privileges), it is possible to locate the SQL to recreate every object in the system. The data dictionary also contains usage information, statistics about the data, and information about the performance of the database. Luckily, ninety percent of what can be done with the data dictionary is outside the scope of this test so it can be ignored in this guide.

All of the data dictionary tables are owned by the SYS account, and tend to have very cryptic names. Few accounts have access to view these tables at all. Querying the tables directly is not recommended and in all but a vanishingly small number of exceptions not worthwhile. The vast majority of the data you need from the data dictionary can be retrieved from views created specifically for the purpose of exposing the information required by users and administrators. A significant number of these views come with one of three prefixes:

- **DBA_** -- These views show data dictionary objects across all schemas. The views are intended to be used by people with Database Administrator-level privileges.
- **ALL_** -- These views show data dictionary objects across multiple schemas. The objects shown are filtered based on object level privileges, however. Objects in schemas other than the user querying the view will only be shown if the user has privileges on the object in the other schema.
- **USER_** – These views show only data dictionary objects that exist in the schema that is performing the query. The USER views lack the OWNER column that exists in the DBA_ and ALL_ views, since the information is redundant.

The majority of the views outside the above three contain performance statistics:

- **V$** -- Dynamic performance views for the local database
- **GV$** -- Global dynamic performance views for multiple instances when utilizing Real Application Clusters.

It's obviously not possible in this book to detail all of the available views. However, some of the more useful views on non-schema objects are:

- **DBA_USERS** -- Information about all users of the database.
- **DICTIONARY** -- Description of data dictionary tables and views.
- **DICT_COLUMNS** -- Description of columns in data dictionary tables and views.
- **GLOBAL_NAME** – Displays the global database name.
- **NLS_DATABASE_PARAMETERS** -- Permanent NLS parameters of the database.
- **SESSION_PRIVS** – Displays all system privileges available in the current session.

Likewise some of the more useful views on schema objects are: (USER views shown, there are DBA and ALL equivalents)

- **USER_INDEXES** -- Describes all indexes in the current schema.
- **USER_IND_COLUMNS** -- Describes the columns of indexes on all tables in the current schema.
- **USER_SEQUENCES** -- Describes all sequences in the current schema.
- **USER_SYNONYMS** -- Describes all synonyms in the current schema.
- **USER_SYS_PRIVS** -- Describes system privileges granted to the current user.
- **USER_TAB_COLUMNS** -- Describes columns of all tables, views, and clusters in the current schema.
- **USER_TAB_PRIVS** -- Describes all object grants in the current schema.

- **USER_TABLES** -- Describes all relational tables in the current schema.
- **USER_OBJECTS** -- Describes all objects in the current schema.

The dynamic performance views are extremely useful for getting information about your database. They display information about your database in real time. The views themselves actually have names that begin with **V_$**, but they each have matching public synonyms that start with **V$**. When using these views, you should be aware that Oracle does not recommend complex queries against them, with or without joins. Because of the dynamic nature of the views, Oracle cannot guarantee read consistency when anything other than simple single-view queries are executed against them. Some of the V$ views are:

- **V$DATABASE** -- This view lets you access information about the database (such as archivelog status).
- **V$DATAFILE** -- This view contains an entry for each datafile of the database.
- **V$NLS_PARAMETERS** -- The NLS parameters that are in effect for the session querying this view.
- **V$PARAMETER** -- Lists the name-value pairs of the init.ora file (or their default, if not in the init.ora).
- **V$SQLTEXT_WITH_NEWLINES** -- This view can be used to construct the entire text for each session's actual SQL statement.
- **V$VERSION** -- Use this view to find out the specific version of the database components.

The USER_TABLES view can provide you with more information about a table than you ever wanted to know. The columns below are just a fraction of the ones available.

```
SELECT table_name, status, pct_free, pct_used,
       num_rows, blocks
FROM   user_tables
WHERE  table_name = 'AIRPORTS';
```

```
TABLE_NAME   STATUS  PCT_FREE PCT_USED NUM_ROWS BLOCKS
------------ ------- -------- -------- -------- ------
AIRPORTS     VALID         10       40        5      1
```

The V$VERSION view is useful for determining exactly which versions of Oracle software the current database is running.

```
SELECT *
FROM   v$version;

BANNER
---------------------------------------------------------------
Oracle Database 11g Express Edition Release 11.2.0.2.0 - Production
PL/SQL Release 11.2.0.2.0 - Production
CORE 11.2.0.2.0    Production
TNS for 32-bit Windows: Version 11.2.0.2.0 - Production
NLSRTL Version 11.2.0.2.0 - Production
```

The DICTIONARY view is an excellent starting point for learning about the data dictionary objects available. The COMMENTS field gives a brief description of the vast majority of objects available.

```
SELECT *
FROM   dictionary
WHERE  table_name LIKE 'USER_COL%'

TABLE_NAME              COMMENTS
----------------------- -------------------------------------
USER_COLL_TYPES         Description of the user's own named
                          collection types
USER_COL_COMMENTS       Comments on columns of user's tables
                          and views
USER_COL_PENDING_STATS  Pending statistics of tables,
                          partitions, and subpartitions
USER_COL_PRIVS_MADE     All grants on columns of objects
                          owned by the user
USER_COL_PRIVS_RECD     Grants on columns for which the
                          user is the grantee
```

# Controlling User Access

## Differentiate system privileges from object privileges

In order for a RDBMS to be a viable platform for enterprise databases, the data must be secure. The sum total of the data within it should not be freely available to anyone that can log in to the database. Oracle maintains security within the database through the use of user privileges. The two most common means of controlling user privileges are:

- Granting and revoking privileges to individual users or groups of users.
- Creating a database role and assigning privileges to it. A role is a named database object to which you grant related privileges. You can then grant that role (and all associated privileges) to users or to other roles.

A third means is through the use of secure application roles. However, that is outside the scope of the test.

There are two broad classes of privileges that can be granted to a user or role:

- **System Privileges** – Provide the ability to perform a task that has a scope beyond that of a single database object. Many of the system privileges have a scope of the entire database, for example ALTER USER or CREATE ROLLBACK SEGMENT. Others have a scope that is just for the schema of the user who has been granted the privilege, for example CREATE TABLE or CREATE PROCEDURE.
- **Object Privileges** – Provide the ability to perform a task on a specific database object. For example, GRANT SELECT ON employees.

Some examples of System Privileges are:

- **CREATE TABLE** -- Create a table in the grantee's schema.
- **CREATE ANY TABLE** -- Create a table in any schema.
- **ALTER ANY TABLE** -- Alter any table or view in any schema.
- **DELETE ANY TABLE** -- Delete rows from tables in any schema.
- **DROP ANY TABLE** -- Drop (or truncate) tables in any schema.
- **INSERT ANY TABLE** -- Insert rows into tables in any schema.
- **CREATE ANY INDEX** Create an index on any table in any schema.
- **ALTER ANY INDEX** Alter indexes in any schema.

Some examples of Object Privileges are:

- **ALTER** – Right to use ALTER TABLE to change a given table.
- **INDEX** – Right to use the CREATE INDEX command on a given table.
- **INSERT** – Right to INSERT new rows into a given table.
- **SELECT** – Right to SELECT data from a given table.
- **UPDATE** – Right to UPDATE data in a given table.
- **DELETE** – Right to use DELETE rows from a given table.

**PUBLIC**

If there is a requirement that every database user have a given privilege, its possible to grant that privilege to PUBLIC. After granting a privilege to PUBLIC, the privilege is freely available to every single database user without exception. This must always be used with caution, especially when dealing with system privileges. System grants to PUBLIC should be avoided as a general rule.

## ANY keyword

A significant percentage of system privileges have two similar commands, with and without the ANY keyword (i.e. CREATE TABLE vs CREATE ANY TABLE). The ANY keyword means that the grant is not schema-specific. When a user is granted CREATE TABLE, they are able to create tables in their own schema. However, when granted CREATE ANY TABLE, they can create tables in any user's schema. The ANY keyword makes the privilege much less restrictive and therefore much more dangerous.

## WITH ADMIN OPTION

System privileges may optionally be made using the WITH ADMIN option (i.e. GRANT ALTER ANY TABLE WITH ADMIN OPTION). This option allows the user granted this privilege to grant it to other users in turn. In fact, they can grant the privilege to a third user 'WITH ADMIN OPTION' who could in turn grant it to a fourth and so on. If the system privilege is later revoked from a user who was given the admin option, any grants they made of this system privilege are not revoked. The revoke of system privileges **does not** cascade.

## WITH GRANT OPTION

Object privileges have a similar clause called the WITH GRANT OPTION. When an object privilege is granted to a user with this option, that user can grant the object privilege to other users. One distinct difference between the two is that if the privilege is revoked from a user given the WITH GRANT OPTION, any privileges that the user granted are also revoked. The revoke of object privileges **does** cascade.

## Grant privileges on tables and on a user

In order to access tables that are owned by another schema, you must have been granted access to do so. This might be through a system privilege such as SELECT ANY TABLE, or by a grant on the table itself by the schema owner, or a schema that has privileges that allow it to grant the required access. Until a privilege has been granted, Oracle will treat attempts to SELECT from it as if the table does not even exist.

```
SELECT *
FROM   hr.regions;

ORA-00942: table or view does not exist
00942. 00000 -  "table or view does not exist"
*Cause:
*Action:
```

If the SELECT privilege is granted to the querying schema, then the above statement will succeed:

```
GRANT SELECT ON hr.regions TO ocpguru;

GRANT succeeded.

SELECT *
FROM   hr.regions;

REGION_ID REGION_NAME
--------- -------------------------
        1 Europe
        2 Americas
        3 Asia
        4 Middle East and Africa
```

To remove a privilege that has been granted, the REVOKE statement is required:

```
REVOKE SELECT ON hr.regions FROM ocpguru;

REVOKE succeeded.
```

There are a number of different privileges beyond SELECT that can be granted to a user. As per the section above, these can be granted as object privileges where they are applicable only for a specific object in the data dictionary or as a system privilege where they cover all objects. Some of these include:

- **DELETE** -- Delete rows in a table.
- **INSERT** -- Insert rows in a table.
- **UPDATE** -- Update data in a table or a subset of columns in a table.
- **REFERENCES** -- Create a foreign key reference on a table or a subset of columns in a table.
- **TRIGGER** -- Create a trigger on a table or a subset of columns in a table.

It is possible to grant multiple privileges in a single statement by providing a comma-separated list. It is also possible to grant one or more privileges to multiple users in the same fashion. The following example grants the UPDATE and DELETE privileges to the users JJONES and NGREENBE:

```
GRANT update, delete ON aircraft_types TO jjones, ngreenbe;
GRANT succeeded.
```

## Distinguish between privileges and roles

A role is a container for a set of privileges. It is not in and of itself a privilege. When created, a new role contains no privileges and granting it to a user would confer no additional rights within the database. Once privileges have been added to a role and the role granted to a user, the user can then enable it and exercise the privileges granted by it.

Privileges granted to a schema are part of that schema even when the user is not logged in to the database. By contrast, the privileges a schema has from a role are only in effect while the user has an open database session (and even then, it is possible to disable a role for a given session).

Although this is outside the scope of the test, I'll note that one consequence of roles being only in effect during a session is that it is not possible to create stored PL/SQL objects that require a privilege granted to a schema via a role. For example, if you had the SELECT privilege on the EMPLOYEES table through a role, you would not be able to create a stored procedure that had a cursor referencing the table (although you could make use of such a cursor in an anonymous PL/SQL block). Since stored PL/SQL procedures might be used when a user is not currently logged into the database, either by another user or through a scheduled job, the rights required by the procedure must be persistent.

# Managing Schema Objects

## Describe how schema objects work

Objects in the Oracle Database fall into two broad classes, schema objects and non-schema objects. If an object is associated with a particular schema, then it is a schema object. Conversely, if not, it is a non-schema object. A database schema is owned by and has the same name as an Oracle database user. The user and schema are not the same thing. However, since they are created simultaneously, cannot exist independently, and dropping a user drops the schema of the same name – the two are often treated as the same thing. The schema itself is defined as a collection of logical structures of data, or objects. Schema objects are created and manipulated via SQL statements. A partial list of schema objects follows:

- Constraints
- Database triggers
- Indexes
- Sequences
- Synonyms
- Tables
- Views

Nonschema Objects are also stored in the database and can be created and manipulated with SQL. However, they are not contained in a schema and (with the exception of users) have no affinity to any particular schema. A partial list of these includes:

- Directories
- Roles
- Rollback segments
- Tablespaces
- Users

Schemas provide for a way to separate the objects of different users. User A stores their tables in Schema A and User B stores their tables in Schema B. This makes it easier for users to keep track of their information and also provides a level of security. By default, users have access only to objects in their own schemas unless the owning user specifically grants them access. Schemas also allow for resource allocation. The database administrator can grant space in tablespaces to each user's schema based on their job role and requirements.

When DML and DDL statements are executed, Oracle always determines what schema is being affected by the statement. Ideally, you should always explicitly define the schema by prefixing the object name with the schema and a period. This makes the intent of the statement perfectly clear by avoiding ambiguity and also means the Oracle does not have to spend parse time determining which schema should be referenced. In practice, however, schemas are left off more often than they are specified. The following statement works:

```
SELECT emp_first, emp_last, emp_job, salary
FROM   employees
WHERE  emp_job = 'SVP';
ORDER BY 2, 1;

EMP_FIRST  EMP_LAST   EMP_JOB    SALARY
---------- ---------- ---------- ------
Rick       Jameson    SVP        145200
Rob        Stoner     SVP        149100
```

Because it works, SQL developers often do not explicitly define the schema:

```
SELECT emp_first, emp_last, emp_job, salary
FROM   ocpguru.employees
WHERE  emp_job = 'SVP';
ORDER BY 2, 1;

EMP_FIRST  EMP_LAST   EMP_JOB    SALARY
---------- ---------- ---------- ------
Rick       Jameson    SVP        145200
Rob        Stoner     SVP        149100
```

When the object being referenced by a DML statement is not in the current schema, however, often it is required that the schema where the object exists be added to the statement. I should note that it is possible to reference objects in different schema without a schema reference if a synonym has been created to the destination object. An Oracle synonym is simply a database object that redirects SQL references against a defined name to a specific schema object. That said, synonyms are not a topic of this exam and so should not appear in questions. You need to understand that schemas provide a container to store database objects, assign privileges and resources, and how to prefix object names with a schema.

## Create simple and complex views with visible/invisible columns

The base difference between simple and complex views is that a simple view selects from a single table and does not aggregate data whereas a complex view selects from more than one table and/or aggregates data. It is possible to perform DML operations against simple views. It **may** be possible to perform DML operations against a complex view, but it is dependent on the particular view.

You cannot delete or modify data via a view if either of the following is true:

- The view has aggregated data.
- The view contains the DISTINCT/UNIQUE keyword

You cannot insert data in a view if either of the above is true, or:

- There are NOT NULL columns in the table that are not selected by the view (unless these columns have a default value defined).

As a general rule you also cannot use DML on a query that contains JOINs. This rule can be circumvented if you have a key preserved table. However, key preserved tables are not an exam topic.

The following example is a simple view. It does not include the salary column from the EMPLOYEES table. Users given SELECT access on this view but *not* the base table will not be able to access employee salary information.

```
CREATE OR REPLACE VIEW employees_no_sal_v
AS
SELECT emp_first, emp_last, emp_job, start_date
FROM   employees;

view EMPLOYEES_NO_SAL_V created.
```

The following example is a complex view. By joining the AIRPORTS and AIRCRAFT_TYPES through the AIRCRAFT_FLEET table, this view allows you to easily query all of the aircraft in the fleet without having to create the joins each time.

```
CREATE OR REPLACE VIEW aircraft_fleet_v
AS
SELECT apt_name, apt_abbr, act_name, act_body_style, act_decks,
act_seats
FROM   airports apt
       INNER JOIN aircraft_fleet afl
       ON apt.apt_id = afl.apt_id
       INNER JOIN aircraft_types act
       ON act.act_id = afl.act_id;

view AIRCRAFT_FLEET_V created.
```

If any columns selected in the view are expressions, then the expression must be provided with an alias in order for a view to be created. The alias must meet normal naming convention rules. The following expands on the EMPLOYEE_NOSAL_V view created above, adding two new columns, one with the employee's full name separated by a space, and the second with their last name then the first name separated by a comma.

```
CREATE OR REPLACE VIEW employees_morenames_v
AS
SELECT emp_first, emp_last, emp_job, start_date,
       emp_first || ' ' || emp_last AS EMP_FULL_NAME,
       emp_last  || ', ' || emp_first AS EMP_LAST_FIRST
FROM   employees;

view EMPLOYEES_MORENAMES_V created.
```

Another syntax for defining the view column names during creation is:

```
CREATE OR REPLACE VIEW employees_morenames_v
   (emp_first, emp_last, emp_job, start_date, emp_full_name,
emp_last_name)
AS
SELECT emp_first, emp_last, emp_job, start_date,
       emp_first || ' ' || emp_last,
       emp_last  || ', ' || emp_first
FROM   employees;

view EMPLOYEES_MORENAMES_V created.
```

### Invisible columns

Just as it is possible to create invisible columns in a table, 12c provides the capability to create invisible columns in a view. The behavior is essentially identical to invisible columns in a table. Invisible columns in a view are only accessible when directly referenced. The following examples make use of INVISO_TEST that was used earlier in this book to demonstrate invisible columns in a table. To recap -- that table was created with three columns: COL1, COL2, and COL3 using the following SQL:

```
CREATE TABLE inviso_test (
col1   NUMBER,
col2   VARCHAR2(20),
col3   VARCHAR2(20) INVISIBLE);
```

If a view is created against this table using the asterisk syntax, the INVISIBLE setting of COL3 will prevent it from being made part of the view. The column cannot be selected from the view even if directly referenced.

```
CREATE VIEW inviso_test_v1
AS
SELECT *
FROM   inviso_test;

View created.

SELECT *
FROM   inviso_test_v1;

      COL1 COL2
---------- -------------
         1 Visible

SELECT col1, col2, col3
FROM   inviso_test_v1;

ERROR at line 1:
ORA-00904: "COL3": invalid identifier

DESC inviso_test_v1

Name Null Type
---- ---- ------------
COL1      NUMBER
COL2      VARCHAR2(20)
```

If the SELECT clause of the CREATE VIEW statement explicitly references an invisible column in the table, the column will be included in the view. However, the view does not inherit the INVISIBLE aspect of the column. When accessing the view, the column is fully visible despite the fact that is invisible at the table level.

```
CREATE VIEW inviso_test_v2
AS
SELECT col1, col2, col3
FROM   inviso_test;

SELECT *
FROM inviso_test_v2;

      COL1 COL2                 COL3
---------- -------------------- --------------------
         1 Visible
         2 Visible              Invisible
```

```
DESC inviso_test_v2

Name Null Type
---- ---- ------------
COL1      NUMBER
COL2      VARCHAR2(20)
COL3      VARCHAR2(20)
```

Any columns created in a view will be VISIBLE regardless of their visibility in the base tables unless they are explicitly marked INVISIBLE in the view definition. In order to make a column invisible in a view, the column names must be specified explicitly in the view definition. The INVISIBLE keyword can be used to make one or more columns invisible in the view regardless of their visibility in the base table. The following example explicitly sets COL3 to INVISIBLE. Its behavior then matches that of the column in the base table.

```
CREATE VIEW inviso_test_v3
(col1, col2, col3 INVISIBLE)
AS
SELECT col1, col2, col3
FROM   inviso_test;


SELECT *
FROM inviso_test_v3;

      COL1 COL2
---------- --------------------
         1 Visible
         2 Visible

DESC inviso_test_v3

Name Null Type
---- ---- ------------
COL1      NUMBER
COL2      VARCHAR2(20)
```

There is no reason that the behavior of the view has to match that of the base table, though. The following example makes a view where COL2 is invisible while leaving COL3 visible. The view then acts quite differently from the base table:

```
CREATE VIEW inviso_test_v4
(col1, col2 INVISIBLE, col3)
AS
SELECT col1, col2, col3
FROM   inviso_test;

SELECT *
FROM inviso_test_v4;

      COL1 COL3
---------- --------------------
         1
         2 Invisible

DESC inviso_test_v4

Name Null Type
---- ---- ------------
COL1      NUMBER
COL3      VARCHAR2(20)
```

## Create, maintain and use sequences

Sequences are database objects from which multiple users may generate unique integers. They are often used to automatically generate primary key values. Every time a sequence number is generated, the value is incremented, independent of whether the transaction is committed or rolled back. If a SQL statement generates an error, it is automatically rolled back, but any sequences incremented by the call will **not** get rolled back to the value they were previously.

One user can never acquire the sequence number that was generated by another user. Once a sequence exists, the CURRVAL and NEXTVAL pseudocolumns are used to access its values. The CURRVAL pseudocolumn returns the current value of the sequence. The NEXTVAL pseudocolumn increments the sequence and returns the new value. The NEXTVAL and CURRVAL pseudocolumns cannot be used as part of a view, or in an aggregate SELECT statement.

Since sequences do nothing more than return an integer when called, there are only a few questions to be answered about them during creation and CREATE SEQUENCE is a fairly simple command:

- **START WITH** – Specifies the first number to be returned by the sequence (default is 1).
- **INCREMENT BY** – Specifies the integer that will be added to the sequence value each time it is called. This number can be positive or negative (default is 1).
- **MINVALUE** – the lowest value that will be returned by the sequence (default is NOMINVALUE).
- **MAXVALUE** – The highest value that will be returned by the sequence (default is NOMAXVALUE).
- **CYCLE** – Determines whether the sequence will cycle through the same set of numbers continuously or not (default is NOCYCLE).
- **CACHE** – Determines whether or not the sequence will cache values in memory for faster retrieval and how many (default is CACHE 20). NOCACHE will turn off sequence caching entirely.

A sequence created with all default values will start at one, and increment by 1 with no maximum value and utilize a cache of 20 values). To create a sequence that stops at a predefined limit, specify a value for the MAXVALUE or MINVALUE parameters (for ascending/descending sequences respectively) and add NOCYCLE. Once the sequence has reached its limit, any further calls to NEXTVAL generate an error.

To create a sequence that restarts after reaching a predefined limit, specify the MAXVALUE and MINVALUE parameters and the CYCLE keyword. When an ascending sequence hits the MAXVALUE, the next call to NEXTVAL will return the number set by MINVALUE. Likewise a descending sequence will step from MINVALUE to the MAXVALUE.

The following example creates a sequence called SEQ_EMP_ID that starts with the number 18, increments by one each time the NEXTVAL pseudocolumn is referenced, and does not cache any values.

```
CREATE SEQUENCE seq_emp_id
START WITH 18
INCREMENT BY 1
NOCACHE;

sequence SEQ_EMP_ID created.
```

Once created, we can pull the next number from the sequence as follows:

```
SELECT seq_emp_id.nextval FROM dual;

NEXTVAL
-------
     18
```

If we were to make the above call a second time, it would return the value 19. However, we can pull the current sequence value without causing it to increment by using the CURRVAL pseudocolumn:

```
SELECT seq_emp_id.currval FROM dual;

CURRVAL
-------
     18
```

## Create and maintain indexes including invisible indexes and multiple indexes on the same columns

Indexes contain an entry for each value that is stored in the indexed column(s) of the table. Each index entry contains a locator to the block(s) in the data file containing the row(s) with that value and provide direct, fast access to them. Tables can have multiple indexes created on them. The tradeoffs involved in creating multiple indexes on the same table are outside the scope of this test. A DML statement that includes an indexed column in a WHERE clause <u>might</u> see a performance benefit. The uncertainty lies in the fact that the Oracle Cost Based Optimizer may or may not choose to make use of the index.

Oracle supports several types of index:

- **Normal indexes** -- The default index type in Oracle is a B-tree index.
- **Bitmap indexes** -- Store the ROWID values associated with a key value as a bitmap. A bitmap index cannot be UNIQUE.
- **Partitioned indexes** -- Consist of partitions containing an entry for each value that appears in the indexed column(s) of the table.
- **Function-based indexes** – Store expressions based on column data rather than the column data itself. They enable you to construct queries that filter by an expression and get the performance benefit of an index.

When creating indexes manually via the CREATE INDEX command, you can index a single column:

```
CREATE INDEX emp_last_ndx
ON employees (emp_last);

index EMP_LAST_NDX created.
```

You can also create a single index that contains multiple columns:

```
CREATE INDEX emp_last_first_ndx
ON employees (emp_last, emp_first);

index EMP_LAST_FIRST_NDX created.
```

Whenever a DML query includes one or more indexed columns in the WHERE clause, the Oracle Cost Based Optimizer has to decide whether or not making use of the index will improve the performance of the operation. The optimizer uses table statistics to try to determine what percentage of rows in the table will be returned by the query. If the answer is most (or all) of the rows in the table, then skipping the index in favor of a full-table scan is likely to be the better option from a performance standpoint. The full scope of the CBO decision-making process is much more complex, but this is a significant part of the decision on using indexes. Indexes are never used when the comparison being performed is '!=', 'NOT IN', or 'IS NULL' or if the column being compared is in a function and the index is not a function-based index (using the same function as is in the WHERE clause).

Oracle maintains indexes automatically. There is no command that you must issue to account for a row being added or deleted, or an indexed value being changed. Every time a table change is made that affects an indexed value, Oracle performs the necessary updates to all affected indexes on that table. The automated work is part of the downside to having multiple indexes on a given table. Multiple indexes **might** improve performance for selects, but they **will** create overhead that reduces performance for inserts, updates and deletes.

The only manual performance operation that you might perform on an index is a rebuild. Index rebuilds can sometimes reduce the size and improve the performance characteristics for an index that has had a lot of data changes since the index was built (or last rebuilt).

```
ALTER INDEX emp_last_first_ndx REBUILD;

index EMP_LAST_FIRST_NDX altered.
```

If you decide that an index is not being used or if you want to replace it with an index created in a different fashion, you can remove it from the data dictionary with the DROP INDEX command. If a table with indexes is dropped, all of the associated indexes will be dropped automatically.

```
DROP INDEX emp_last_first_ndx;

index EMP_LAST_FIRST_NDX dropped.
```

### Indexes and Constraints

The two constraints that make use of indexes for enforcement are PRIMARY KEY and UNIQUE constraints. If you add one of these two constraints to a table then an index will be required for the constraint to create successfully. If there is not already an appropriate unique index on the column(s) the constraint is for, an index will be added to the table to enforce the constraint. We can find the index created earlier for the aircraft_types primary key by querying the USER_INDEXES view:

```
SELECT table_name, index_name
FROM   user_indexes
WHERE  table_name = 'AIRCRAFT_TYPES';

TABLE_NAME                 INDEX_NAME
------------------------- -------------
AIRCRAFT_TYPES             SYS_C006988
```

When defining the state of the constraint, you can specify an existing index for Oracle to use for enforcement, or you can instruct Oracle to create a new index, or neither. The three possible options are:

- If you specify USING schema.index, then Oracle attempts to use the specified index. If Oracle cannot find the index or cannot use the index to enforce the constraint an error will be returned.
- If you specify the create_index_statement, then Oracle attempts to create the index and use it to enforce the constraint. If Oracle cannot create the index or cannot use the index to enforce the constraint, then an error is returned.
- If you neither specify an existing index nor create a new index, then Oracle creates the index automatically and generates a unique (and ugly) name for the new index.

Earlier, we added a UNIQUE constraint to the airports table with this statement:

```
ALTER TABLE airports MODIFY (apt_abbr
  CONSTRAINT airport_codes_uk
  UNIQUE USING INDEX airport_codes_uk);
```

An alternate syntax that would have identical results is:

```
ALTER TABLE airports
  ADD CONSTRAINT airport_codes_uk
  UNIQUE (apt_abbr) USING INDEX airport_codes_uk;
```

If a unique index does not already exist on AIRPORTS.APT_ABBR, then one can be created explicitly as part of the ALTER TABLE statement that creates the constraint:

```
ALTER TABLE airports
  ADD CONSTRAINT airport_codes_uk
  UNIQUE (apt_abbr) USING INDEX
  (CREATE UNIQUE INDEX apt_abbr_uk
   ON airports(apt_abbr));
```

If you add a UNIQUE constraint and provide a constraint name but no USING clause, an index with the same name as the constraint will be created automatically.

```
ALTER TABLE airports
  ADD CONSTRAINT airport_codes_uk
  UNIQUE (apt_abbr);
```

If you add a UNIQUE constraint and provide no constraint name or USING clause, and no index exists that could be used to enforce the constraint, an index will be created automatically. The index and the constraint will be given a system-generated name.

```
ALTER TABLE airports
  ADD UNIQUE (apt_abbr);

table AIRPORTS altered.

SELECT index_name, index_type, uniqueness
FROM   user_indexes
WHERE  table_name = 'AIRPORTS';

INDEX_NAME     INDEX_TYPE     UNIQUENESS
-------------  -------------  ----------
SYS_C007010    NORMAL         UNIQUE
```

## Invisible Indexes

It is possible to create (or alter) indexes that are invisible to the Oracle Optimizer. Invisible indexes are structurally identical to normal indexes and are maintained by the database as rows in the indexed table are added, updated or deleted. However, the index will never be used by the optimizer when accessing data by default. The parameter OPTIMIZER_USE_INVISIBLE_INDEXES can be set to TRUE at the instance or session level to allow the optimizer to make use of invisible indexes (the default is FALSE). Since making an index invisible seems to violate the whole reason they exist, one might ask "What's the point?". Good question. Oracle gives the following three reasons for creating an invisible index:

- Test the removal of an index before dropping it.
- Use temporary index structures for certain operations or modules of an application without affecting the overall application.
- Add an index to a set of columns on which an index already exists.

Whatever the reason for creating them, the following example creates an invisible index directly via the CREATE INDEX statement:

```
CREATE INDEX ac_fleet_act_inv_ndx ON aircraft_fleet(act_id)
INVISIBLE;
index AC_FLEET_ACT_INV_NDX created.
```

The following example creates an index as VISIBLE, then alters it to invisible using the ALTER INDEX statement:

```
CREATE INDEX ac_fleet_apt_inv_ndx ON aircraft_fleet(apt_id);
index AC_FLEET_APT_INV_NDX created.

ALTER INDEX ac_fleet_apt_inv_ndx INVISIBLE;
index AC_FLEET_APT_INV_NDX altered.
```

Finally, it is possible to make an invisible index visible with the ALTER INEX statement:

```
ALTER INDEX ac_fleet_apt_inv_ndx VISIBLE;
index AC_FLEET_APT_INV_NDX altered.
```

**Multiple indexes on the same column**

Until 11g it was not possible to have more than one index on a single column. The same column could appear in more than one index if one or more was a multi-column index (i.e. index A was for column1, index B was for column1 and column 2). However, a given column or set of columns could only have a single index. One of the spinoffs of invisible indexes is that they make it possible to create multiple indexes on the same column (or column set). If you are uncertain what type of index will provide the best performance in a situation, you might create two or more indexes on a given column of different types (such as B-Tree vs bitmap or partitioned vs unpartitioned). When more than a single index exists for a given set of columns, only one can be visible at any given time. Multiple indexes can be created on the same set of columns when at least one of the following index characteristics is different:

- The indexes are of different types, such as B-Tree and Bitmap.
- The indexes use different partitioning logic -- such as one partitioned and the other non-partitioned or one globally partitioned and the other locally partitioned.
- The indexes have different uniqueness properties (i.e. one is UNIQUE and the other is not).

## Perform flashback operations

In release 11g, Oracle introduced a number of features under the umbrella of flashback functionality. The capabilities are implemented and accessed via a number of different methods. The common factor between them is that all of them allow you to access data and or database objects as they existed at an earlier point in time without having to perform media recovery of the database. Capabilities of Oracle Flashback include:

- Performing queries that return past data.
- Performing queries that return metadata with a history of changes to the database.
- Recover tables or rows to a previous point in time.
- Automatically create an archive of transactional data changes.
- Roll back a transaction and its dependent transactions.

The scope of flashback capabilities is significant and many of the functions are linked more closely to recovery and DBA level operations than to SQL queries. In this guide, we'll cover the three aspects most likely to appear on the test: Flashback Query, Flashback Version Query, and Flashback Transaction Query.

## Oracle Flashback Query

Flashback Query is used to retrieve data for a time in the past that is specified using the AS OF clause in a SELECT statement. When the AS OF clause is included in a query and references a past time through a timestamp or System Change Number (SCN), Oracle returns committed data that existed in the database at that point in time. You can use this to recover lost data or reverse committed changes. You can also use the results to compare current data with past data.

The example below demonstrates recovery of an accidentally deleted row using Oracle Flashback Query:

```
DELETE FROM employees
WHERE  emp_last = 'Stoneflint';

1 rows deleted.


SELECT *
FROM   employees
WHERE emp_last = 'Stoneflint';

no rows selected
```

```
SELECT emp_id, emp_first, emp_last, emp_job, salary
FROM   employees
  AS OF TIMESTAMP
   TO_TIMESTAMP('29-MAR-12 11.00.00 PM',
                'DD-MON-YY HH:MI:SS AM')
     WHERE emp_last = 'Stoneflint';

EMP_ID EMP_FIRST EMP_LAST   EMP_JOB SALARY
------ --------- ---------- ------- -------
     7 Fred      Stoneflint SrDir    111500
```

```
INSERT INTO employees
(SELECT *
FROM   employees
  AS OF TIMESTAMP
   TO_TIMESTAMP('29-MAR-12 11.00.00 PM',
                'DD-MON-YY HH:MI:SS AM')
     WHERE emp_last = 'Stoneflint');

1 rows inserted.
```

```
SELECT emp_id, emp_first, emp_last, emp_job, salary
FROM   employees
WHERE emp_last = 'Stoneflint';

EMP_ID EMP_FIRST EMP_LAST   EMP_JOB SALARY
------ --------- ---------- ------- -------
     7      Fred Stoneflint SrDir    111500
```

When utilizing a timestamp in the AS OF clause, Oracle converts the timestamp to an SCN within a 3-second range. If you need to have absolute accuracy on the query, you can use an SCN in the AS OF query instead of a timestamp. If you specify SCN, then the supplied expression must evaluate to a number.

```
SELECT emp_id, emp_first, emp_last, emp_job, salary
FROM   employees
  AS OF SCN 392611
WHERE emp_last = 'Stoneflint';

EMP_ID EMP_FIRST EMP_LAST   EMP_JOB SALARY
------ --------- ---------- ------- -------
     7 Fred      Stoneflint SrDir    111500
```

It's possible to specify a relative time when using the AS OF clause. The example below creates a view that will always return data as it existed three hours in the past.

```
CREATE VIEW employees_minus3_hours_v AS
SELECT * FROM employees
AS OF TIMESTAMP (SYSTIMESTAMP - INTERVAL '180' MINUTE);

view EMPLOYEES_MINUS3_HOURS_V created.
```

**Oracle Flashback Version Query**

Flashback Version Query is used to retrieve metadata and historical data for a specific interval. The interval can be specified by two timestamps or by two SCNs. The metadata returned includes the start and end time a version existed, type of DML operation used to create it, and the identity of the transaction that created each row version. The VERSIONS BETWEEN clause of a SELECT statement is used to generate a Flashback Version Query. The syntax of the VERSIONS BETWEEN clause is: VERSIONS {BETWEEN {SCN | TIMESTAMP} start AND end}.

The Pseudocolumns returned by a Flashback version query are:

- **VERSIONS_START[SCN/TIME]** -- Starting System Change Number (SCN) or TIMESTAMP when the row version was created. NULL if version is from before the start value.
- **VERSIONS_END[SCN/TIME]** -- SCN or TIMESTAMP when the row version expired. If NULL, then either the row version was current at the time of the query or the row is for a DELETE operation.
- **VERSIONS_XID** -- Identifier of the transaction that created the row version.
- **VERSIONS_OPERATION** -- Operation performed by the transaction: I for insertion, D for deletion, or U for update. The version is that of the row that was inserted, deleted, or updated.

A given row version is valid starting at VERSIONS_START* up to, but not including, VERSIONS_END*. That is, it is valid for any time 't' such that VERSIONS_START* <= t < VERSIONS_END*. The following three updates were issued against the EMPLOYEES table, with a pause in-between.

```
UPDATE employees SET salary = 97000
WHERE emp_last='McCoy';
UPDATE employees SET salary = 102000
WHERE emp_last='McCoy';
UPDATE employees SET salary = 105000
WHERE emp_last='McCoy';
COMMIT;
```

Then the following Flashback Versions query was run against employees:

```
SELECT versions_starttime, versions_endtime,
       versions_xid, versions_operation AS OP,
       salary
  FROM employees
  VERSIONS BETWEEN TIMESTAMP
      TO_TIMESTAMP('29-MAR-12 11.46.00PM','DD-MON-YY HH:MI:SSAM')
  AND TO_TIMESTAMP('29-MAR-12 11.52.00PM','DD-MON-YY HH:MI:SSAM')
  WHERE emp_last = 'McCoy';
```

```
VERSIONS_STARTTIME   VERSIONS_ENDTIME      VERSIONS_XID     OP SALARY
-------------------- --------------------- ---------------- -- ------
29-MAR-12 11.51.08PM                       09000900A9010000 U  105000
29-MAR-12 11.49.50PM 29-MAR-12 11.51.08PM 04001A003F010000 U  102000
29-MAR-12 11.49.02PM 29-MAR-12 11.49.50PM 03002100A2010000 U   97000
                     29-MAR-12 11.49.02PM                      93500
```

From the results above, you see the three updates against the table, each increasing the salary column value. It's clear when each salary value started and ended (save the initial value for which the start time was outside the window, and the end value which is current (and therefore has no end time). You can use VERSIONS_XID with Oracle Flashback Transaction Query to locate the metadata for any of the three transactions. This will include the SQL required to undo the row change and the user responsible for the change.

## Oracle Flashback Transaction Query.

A Flashback Transaction Query is used to retrieve metadata and historical data for a single transaction or for all transactions in a supplied interval. The data is generated from the static data dictionary view FLASHBACK_TRANSACTION_QUERY. The Flashback Transaction Query creates a column UNDO_SQL. The SQL text in this field is the logical opposite of the DML operation performed by the transaction shown. The code from this field can usually reverse original transaction within reason (e.g. a SQL_UNDO INSERT operation would be unlikely to insert a row back at the same ROWID from which it was deleted). As a general rule, Oracle Flashback Transaction Query is used in conjunction with an Oracle Flashback Version Query that provides transaction IDs.

```
SELECT operation, start_scn, commit_scn, logon_user
  FROM flashback_transaction_query
    WHERE xid = HEXTORAW('09000900A9010000');

OPERATION     START_SCN COMMIT_SCN LOGON_USER
------------ --------- ---------- ------------
UNKNOWN         393394     393463 OCPGURU
BEGIN           393394     393463 OCPGURU
```

The following statement uses Oracle Flashback Version Query as a subquery to associate each row version with the LOGON_USER responsible for the row data change.

```
SELECT xid, logon_user
  FROM flashback_transaction_query
    WHERE xid IN (
      SELECT versions_xid
      FROM employees VERSIONS BETWEEN TIMESTAMP
        TO_TIMESTAMP('29-MAR-12 11.40.00 PM',
                     'DD-MON-YY HH:MI:SS AM') AND
        TO_TIMESTAMP('29-MAR-12 11.56.00 PM',
                     'DD-MON-YY HH:MI:SS AM')
     );
```

# Manipulating Large Data Sets

## Describe the features of multitable INSERTs

A multitable INSERT statement allows you to conditionally insert rows returned by a subquery into one or more tables. They're often used in Extract-Transform-Load (ETL) processes when populating data warehouses. They can provide a significant performance enhancement over performing multiple individual INSERT operations.

The different types of multitable inserts are:

- **Conditional INSERT FIRST** – Each row returned by the subquery is inserted into the first table for which it matches the condition.
- **Unconditional INSERT ALL** – Each row returned by the subquery is inserted into every target table.
- **Conditional INSERT ALL** – Each row returned by the subquery is inserted into every target table for which it matches the condition.
- **Pivot INSERT** – A variant of the Unconditional INSERT ALL that performs a pivot operation on the data during the insert – turning data from multiple columns in the source subquery into multiple rows in the destination table.

The syntax for a multitable INSERT is:

```
INSERT [conditional_insert_clause]
[insert_into_clause value_clause]
(subquery)
```

The syntax of the conditional_insert_clause is:

```
[ALL] [FIRST]
[WHEN condition THEN] [insert_into_clause value_clause]
[ELSE] [insert_into_clause value_clause]
```

When the ALL keyword is used, the operation will insert a row into every table for which it matches the condition. When the FIRST keyword is used, the operation will insert a row only into the first table for which it matches the condition. If the ALL keyword is used and no conditions are supplied, then every row returned by the subquery will be inserted into every table supplied in the INSERT statement. On a conditional INSERT, if a row does not evaluate to TRUE on any of the conditions and there is no ELSE, then no action is taken for that row. Multitable inserts cannot be performed on views or remote tables.

## Conditional INSERT FIRST

The Conditional INSERT FIRST statement steps through the values returned by the subquery. As each row is returned, it is evaluated against the conditions from the top down. As soon as one of the conditions evaluate to TRUE, the row will be inserted into the appropriate table. Oracle will skip any remaining insertion conditions and begin evaluating the next row returned by the subquery. The example below conditionally inserts employees records into tables indicating they've been with the company >20 years, >15 years, >10 years, or >5 years.

```
INSERT FIRST
  WHEN MONTHS_BETWEEN(SYSDATE, start_date) >= 240 THEN
    INTO emps_20
    VALUES (emp_id, emp_first, emp_last)
  WHEN MONTHS_BETWEEN(SYSDATE, start_date) >= 180 THEN
    INTO emps_15
    VALUES (emp_id, emp_first, emp_last)
  WHEN MONTHS_BETWEEN(SYSDATE, start_date) >= 120 THEN
    INTO emps_10
    VALUES (emp_id, emp_first, emp_last)
  WHEN MONTHS_BETWEEN(SYSDATE, start_date) >= 60 THEN
    INTO emps_5
    VALUES (emp_id, emp_first, emp_last)
SELECT emp_id, emp_first, emp_last, start_date
FROM   employees;
```

```
SELECT * FROM emps_5;

EMP_ID EMP_FIRST  EMP_LAST
------ ---------- ----------
     6 Janet      Jeckson
    15 Luke       Skytalker
    16 Dell       Aptop
    17 Noh        Kia


SELECT * FROM emps_10;

EMP_ID EMP_FIRST  EMP_LAST
------ ---------- ----------
     8 Alf        Alien
     9 Norm       Storm
    13 James      Thomas
    14 John       Picard
     7 Fred       Stoneflint

SELECT * FROM emps_15;

EMP_ID EMP_FIRST  EMP_LAST
------ ---------- ----------
     1 Big        Boss
     2 Adam       Smith
     3 Rick       Jameson
     4 Rob        Stoner
     5 Bill       Abong
    10 John       Jones
    11 Top        Gun
    12 Phil       McCoy

SELECT * FROM emps_20;

no rows selected
```

## Unconditional INSERT ALL

The following inserts into the EMP_JOBS and EMP_EMAIL tables all rows returned by the subquery. The column values being inserted into the individual tables do not have to match. Every row returned by the subquery results in two table insertions. In the below example, the employee EMAIL and JOB_ID values are broken out into two new tables due to a new and incomprehensible HR requirement.

```
INSERT ALL
    INTO emp_jobs (employee_id, job_id)
    VALUES (employee_id, job_id)
    INTO emp_email (employee_id, email)
    VALUES (employee_id, email)
SELECT employee_id, job_id, email
FROM   hr.employees;

214 rows inserted.


SELECT * FROM emp_jobs WHERE employee_id < 110;

EMPLOYEE_ID JOB_ID
----------- ----------
        100 AD_PRES
        101 AD_VP
        102 AD_VP
        103 IT_PROG
        104 IT_PROG
        105 IT_PROG
        106 IT_PROG
        107 IT_PROG
        108 FI_MGR
        109 FI_ACCOUNT


SELECT * FROM emp_email WHERE employee_id < 110;

EMPLOYEE_ID EMAIL
----------- -------------------------
        100 SKING
        101 NKOCHHAR
        102 LDEHAAN
        103 AHUNOLD
        104 BERNST
        105 DAUSTIN
        106 VPATABAL
        107 DLORENTZ
        108 NGREENBE
        109 DFAVIET
```

## Conditional INSERT ALL

The conditional INSERT ALL simply adds a condition that must be evaluated before the insertion occurs. As each row is returned by the subquery, Oracle checks it against the condition to see if it evaluates to TRUE. If so, it will be inserted. If not, Oracle will move to the next condition or to the next subquery row if no more conditions exist. The following query splits up all of the employees evenly among two teams for a company-wide morale-building game of football.

```
INSERT ALL
  WHEN  MOD(ROWNUM,2) = 1 THEN
    INTO emp_shirts (emp_id, emp_first, emp_last)
    VALUES (emp_id, emp_first, emp_last)
  WHEN  MOD(ROWNUM,2) = 0 THEN
    INTO emp_skins (emp_id, emp_first, emp_last)
    VALUES (emp_id, emp_first, emp_last)
SELECT emp_id, emp_first, emp_last
FROM   employees;

17 rows inserted.


SELECT * FROM emp_shirts;

EMP_ID EMP_FIRST  EMP_LAST
------ ---------- ----------
     1 Big        Boss
     3 Rick       Jameson
     5 Bill       Abong
     8 Alf        Alien
    10 John       Jones
    12 Phil       McCoy
    14 John       Picard
    16 Dell       Aptop
     7 Fred       Stoneflint

SELECT * FROM emp_skins;

EMP_ID EMP_FIRST  EMP_LAST
------ ---------- ----------
     2 Adam       Smith
     4 Rob        Stoner
     6 Janet      Jeckson
     9 Norm       Storm
    11 Top        Gun
    13 James      Thomas
    15 Luke       Skytalker
    17 Noh        Kia
```

## Pivot INSERT

A Pivot INSERT is used to convert column data in the source subquery into row data in the destination table. Converting columns to rows is generally known as a pivot operation. In the example below, the subquery is run against the SALES_BY_FY table. This table contains sales data for various fiscal years with the numbers broken into columns by quarter. The Pivot INSERT operation will use the source data to pull the quarterly sales data out into individual rows to the SALES_BY_QUARTER table.

```
DESC sales_by_fy

Name        Null Type
----------- ---- -----------
FISCAL_YEAR      VARCHAR2(5)
Q1_SALES         NUMBER
Q2_SALES         NUMBER
Q3_SALES         NUMBER
Q4_SALES         NUMBER

SELECT * FROM sales_by_fy;

FISCAL_YEAR Q1_SALES Q2_SALES Q3_SALES Q4_SALES
----------- -------- -------- -------- --------
2010          250000   300000   175000   180000
2011          225000   280000   195000   189000
2012          270000   310000   187000   192000


INSERT ALL
  INTO sales_by_quarter VALUES (fiscal_year, 1, q1_sales)
  INTO sales_by_quarter VALUES (fiscal_year, 2, q2_sales)
  INTO sales_by_quarter VALUES (fiscal_year, 3, q3_sales)
  INTO sales_by_quarter VALUES (fiscal_year, 4, q4_sales)
  SELECT fiscal_year, q1_sales, q2_sales, q3_sales, q4_sales
  FROM   sales_by_fy;


SELECT *
FROM sales_by_quarter
ORDER BY fiscal_year, quarter;
```

```
FISCAL_YEAR QUARTER SALES
----------- ------- -----
2010              1 250000
2010              2 300000
2010              3 175000
2010              4 180000
2011              1 225000
2011              2 280000
2011              3 195000
2011              4 189000
2012              1 270000
2012              2 310000
2012              3 187000
2012              4 192000
```

## Merge rows in a table

MERGE is a DML operation that combines aspects of INSERT, UPDATE and DELETE. A single MERGE statement can perform one, two, or all three activities conditionally. There is nothing that can be performed by the MERGE statement that cannot be performed individually by a combination of INSERT, UPDATE and DELETE operations. The power of a MERGE statement is in being able to perform multiple activities in a single pass. For ETL activities in particular, a MERGE might be able to significantly improve performance on operations involving a large amount of data. In order to perform MERGE operations, you must have the neccesary rights. There is no MERGE privilege – so you need, SELECT, UPDATE, and DELETE privileges on the appropriate tables in order to perform MERGE operations. The syntax for the MERGE statement is:

```
MERGE INTO dest_table tab_alias1
  USING (source_expr) tab_alias2
  ON (join_condition)
   WHEN MATCHED THEN
    UPDATE SET
      col1 = val1,
      col2 = val2
    DELETE WHERE (del_cond)
    WHEN NOT MATCHED THEN
      INSERT (col_list)
      VALUES (col_values)
```

- **dest_table** – The table for which rows will be inserted, updated, or deleted
- **source_expr** – The source of row data for the MERGE, this can be a table, view, or subquery.
- **join_condition** – The condition which is evaluated for each row.
- **del_cond** – Delete row if this condition is met.
- **WHEN MATCHED** – The operation in this clause will be performed when join_condition evaluates to TRUE.
- **WHEN NOT MATCHED** -- The operation in this clause will be performed when join_condition evaluates to FALSE.

An example of this operation follows. The statement is designed to update a backup table to the employees table to match the original. Where employee ids match between the two tables, the backup EMP_ID record is updated to match all the current values in the primary table. Where the employee ID does not exist in the backup, it is inserted directly from the primary.

```
MERGE INTO employees_bkup empb
USING (SELECT * FROM employees) emp
ON (empb.emp_id = emp.emp_id)
WHEN MATCHED THEN
UPDATE SET
  empb.afl_id = emp.afl_id,
  empb.emp_first = emp.emp_first,
  empb.emp_last = emp.emp_last,
  empb.emp_job = emp.emp_job,
  empb.emp_supervisor = emp.emp_supervisor,
  empb.salary = emp.salary,
  empb.start_date = emp.start_date
WHEN NOT MATCHED THEN
INSERT VALUES (emp.emp_id, emp.afl_id, emp.emp_first, emp.emp_last,
     emp.emp_job, emp.emp_supervisor, emp.salary, emp.start_date);
```

A MERGE statement cannot alter the column that is referenced in the join condition of the ON clause.

# ABOUT THE AUTHOR

Matthew Morris is an Oracle Database Administrator and Developer currently employed as a Database Engineer with Computer Sciences Corporation. Matthew has worked with the Oracle database since 1996 when he worked in the RDBMS support team for Oracle Support Services. Employed with Oracle for over eleven years in support and development positions, Matthew was an early adopter of the Oracle Certified Professional program. He was one of the first one hundred Oracle Certified Database Administrators (version 7.3) and in the first hundred to become an Oracle Certified Forms Developer. In the years since, he has upgraded his Database Administrator certification for releases 8i, 9i, 10g, 11g and 12c, become an Oracle Advanced PL/SQL Developer Certified Professional and added the Expert certifications for Application Express, SQL, and SQL Tuning.

Printed in Great Britain
by Amazon